S0-BZP-368

HOW TO AVOID LOVE AND MARRIAGE

Illustrations by Dan Greenburg
Illustrations conceived by Dan Greenburg and Suzanne O'Malley

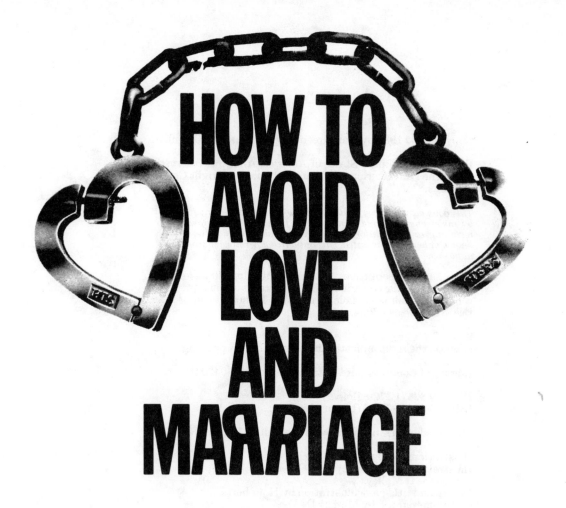

HOW TO AVOID LOVE AND MARRIAGE

Dan Greenburg and Suzanne O'Malley

RUNNING PRESS
PHILADELPHIA, PENNSYLVANIA

Copyright © 1983 by Dan Greenburg and Suzanne O'Malley.

Printed in the United States of America. All rights reserved under the Pan-American and International Copyright Conventions.

This book may not be reproduced in whole or in part in any form or by any means electronic or mechanical, including photocopying, recording, or by any information storage and retrieval system now known or hereafter invented, without written permission from the publisher.

Canadian representatives: General Publishing, 30 Lesmill Road, Don Mills, Ontario M3B 2T6. International representatives: Kaiman & Polon, Inc., 2175 Lemoine Avenue, Fort Lee, New Jersey 07024.

9   8   7   6   5   4   3   2   1
Digit on the right indicates the number of this printing.

Library of Congress Card Catalog Number: 85-043045

ISBN: 0-89471-372-8 (Paper)
ISBN: 0-89471-373-6 (Library binding)

Published by arrangement with Freundlich Books, New York.

Illustrations by Dan Greenburg.
Illustrations conceived by Dan Greenburg and
    Suzanne O'Malley.
Design and title page illustration by H. Roberts.
Cover photograph by Marcus De Voe.
Bridal dress designed by Mariann Marlowe,
    611 Broadway, New York City.
Bridal headpiece by Frank Olive.
Bridal bouquet by Beekman Florist Ltd.

This book can be ordered by mail from the publisher. Please include $1.00 for postage. **But try your bookstore first!** Running Press Book Publishers, 125 South 22nd Street, Philadelphia, Pennsylvania 19103.

Contents

WHY DO YOU NEED
THIS BOOK?

In the middle of a fight with your beloved, do you ever catch yourself saying something so preposterous you want to burst out laughing?

Are you smart enough to know when you're engaging in childish, relationship-destroying behavior with your boyfriend, girlfriend, or spouse, but too stubborn to stop?

Well, then, this book is for you. Because you know that as nice as it is to be in a romantic relationship, you will always find a way to screw it up. Why? Because getting too close to somebody isn't comfortable. You get too close to a lover or spouse, the next thing you know, you feel like you're committed to them forever and you no longer have the option of sliding into a better relationship if Miss Right or Mr. Right happens to come along. You get too close to a lover or spouse, you get really open and loving and vulnerable, and the next thing you know you get dumped for somebody else. You get too close to a lover or a spouse, and you might just have to sabotage the relationship to prevent this sort of thing from happening.

You may say you want to remain uncommitted. Or you may desperately wish to be committed—if only you could find someone who suits you. You may feel it's best to keep your options open. Or you may be the kind of person who claims not to have any *decent* options—but would settle down in a second if you did. Your disillusionment may even be so great that you've decided it's best to avoid love and marriage entirely.

Who are you kidding? Are you going to believe your own hogwash? Do you really *want* to spend the rest of your life with nobody to love you and probably die alone in bed in the middle of the night and not have your body discovered until the next hot spell? All right, then.

That's why you need this book.

This book is devoted to that remote little part of you that is going to rescue you from growing old alone. The part that is willing to laugh when you say something preposterous or to admit it when you act like a stubborn child. The part whose sole responsibility is to save you from yourself.

If, somewhere in these pages on the subject of love and marriage, you experience the shock of recognition—don't be alarmed. No one has to know that you suddenly see how you've been pushing your mate—or potential mates—away. Keep it between you and that pesky little part of you that's always on your case.

Read on!

HOW TO AVOID LOVE AND MARRIAGE

SEXUAL ATTRACTIVENESS OF VARIOUS FEMALES* COMPARED

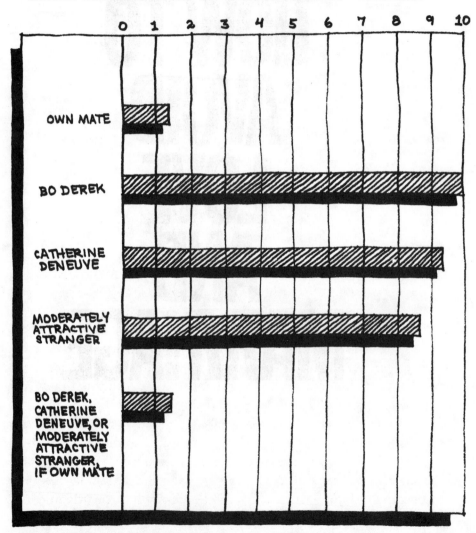

* Note: For males substitute Robert Redford and Warren Beatty.

How to Avoid Love as a Single Person

NATURAL AND HISTORICAL
ORIGINS OF MARRIAGE

Before committing yourself to one mate for the rest of your life in marriage, it is interesting to reflect briefly on the natural and historical implications of marriage. Marriage, you'll remember, is not really a natural state. In nature, coupling is almost always for the sole purpose of mating. Few members of the animal kingdom stay together in couples after mating, except for carrier pigeons and whales. Are you going to stay together with one mate because of carrier pigeons and whales?

The custom of marriage was originally created to protect the property rights of clan patriarchs to holdings of land and cattle. Is this a valid reason for you to commit yourself to a single mate for the rest of your life—and share a checking account— because a bunch of old guys with long white beards and dirty robes were afraid of losing some land in the desert and a bunch of sheep and donkeys? Get *serious!*

---------------- ♥ ----------------

APTITUDE TEST:
SELECTING THE PROSPECTIVE MATE

Pause a moment now and give yourself this test before reading further.

Which of the following are good prospects for serious romantic relationships, which bad, and why?

1. A man who lives in another city.
　　　☐ GOOD ☐ BAD

2. A woman who hooks part-time.
　　　☐ GOOD ☐ BAD

3. An alcoholic guy who consumes a quart of booze a day, but who is planning to give up drinking.
　　　☐ GOOD ☐ BAD

4. A suicidal woman who has tried it unsuccessfully twice.
　　　☐ GOOD ☐ BAD

5. A married man who is not happy at home and plans to split as soon as he can break it to his wife.
　　　☐ GOOD ☐ BAD

6. A man who's been divorced three times.
　　　☐ GOOD ☐ BAD

7. A girl at least fifteen years younger than you.

☐ GOOD ☐ BAD

8. A mature woman who makes a good living.

☐ GOOD ☐ BAD

9. A guy who's a terrific dancer but who can't seem to hold a job.

☐ GOOD ☐ BAD

10. A very beautiful girl who isn't too interesting to talk to.

☐ GOOD ☐ BAD

Answers:

1. Good. You won't see each other enough to get bored.

2. Good. She has a decent income, and could probably teach you a few tricks in bed.

3. Good. If he says he'll give it up, he will.

4. Good. The fact that she was unsuccessful indicates she wasn't serious about it.

5. Good. You can help by telling him how to do it.

6. Good. He's probably learned his lesson by now and is ready to settle down permanently.

7. Good. She is naïve enough to be impressed with your experience.

8. Bad. She probably makes more than you do and will be contemptuous.

9. Good. Maybe he could dance professionally, like in a play on Broadway or something.
10. Good. Every guy you know will be impressed. Besides, who needs to talk? When you run out of things to talk about, you can always just stare at her.

If you thought more than six of the above were bad prospects for serious romantic relationships, you're in worse shape than we thought. Perhaps you're still looking for Mr. Right or Miss Right. If so, the following section will help you clarify the situation.

--------------- ♥ ---------------

HOW TO SPOT MR. RIGHT

Mr. Right is handsome, sexy, intelligent, and successful. He works hard but knows how to have fun. He is at ease with himself, dresses well, has a great sense of humor and is incredibly romantic, without being sappy. Unfortunately for you, Mr. Right is going with someone else.

That's always the way it is—the really good guys are all taken. There are those few times, of course, when Mr. Right has suddenly become available. The discouraging thing is, the minute *you* begin to date him he changes completely. He's nothing like what he was when he was unavailable. First, you notice he's starting to lose his looks—maybe even some hair. Then, he de-

CONCENTRATION OF AVAILABLE MEN IN CONTINENTAL UNITED STATES

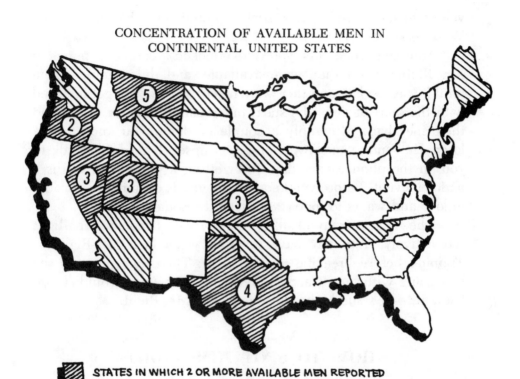

STATES IN WHICH 2 OR MORE AVAILABLE MEN REPORTED

STATES IN WHICH LESS THAN 2 AVAILABLE MEN REPORTED

STATES IN WHICH LESS THAN 1 AVAILABLE MAN REPORTED

SOURCE: AVAILABLE WOMEN

velops financial and career problems and loses his savoir-faire. Who needs it?

You have to confess, you've overlooked a couple of potential Mr. Rights when they were available, and didn't notice them until it was too late and they were taken. Mostly, you get involved with the kind of guy who starts out seeming like Mr. Right and then goes bad. After only a couple of dates, you know he's a loser. He sends you flowers and gets upset if he doesn't talk to you on the phone every day. Just getting a pizza with you is a national event. Before you know it, the guy is claiming he's madly in love and wants to marry you. How tiresome.

The biggest irony of all is the guy who becomes Mr. Right retroactively. You may have invested years in a Mr.-Right-in-Training before breaking up with him. Then, one day you see he's going with an attractive friend of yours and—wouldn't you know it?—he's suddenly blossomed into Mr. Right.

HOW TO SPOT MISS RIGHT

A potential Miss Right is easy enough to spot. She's a model or an actress—or possibly a stewardess. She's the most beautiful and vivacious woman in the room, and you are afraid that you don't make enough money, have good enough looks, or aren't suave enough to interest her.

The key word here is *potential* Miss Right. Even if you've been lucky enough to succeed in your initial conquest of a potential Miss Right, you can't be sure she really *is* Miss Right. Whereas a real Miss Right remains consistently perfect, a potential Miss Right develops fat thighs after you've been to bed with her once or twice. Sometimes, though, just when you're sure a potential Miss Right is bogus, you learn she's going out with someone else, and her thighs shape right up again. Who can tell?

It's a travesty: you can never positively identify an authentic Miss Right until after you lose her. You'd think there'd be a better system.

All the same, that's the way it is. She loved you, adored you, was devoted to you. And what did you do? You pushed her away, tested her, cheated on her with other women. She knew you for the awful person you really are, and she *still* loved you! Who's going to love you now? God, you haven't felt this bad since you were four and your mother left you at home and went to Bermuda on vacation with your father.

----------- ♥ -----------

DEVELOPING RAW MATERIAL

Miss Right or Mr. Right may have their good points, but it is sometimes preferable to work with someone's potential rather than to get a ready-made person who's set in his or her ways. So often you'll find a mate who is perfect except for one or two minor flaws, but these can easily be corrected under your expert tutelage.

Here are a few suggestions for developing raw material:

1. Get a married man to leave his wife for you.
2. Get a married woman to leave her husband for you.
3. Reform a homosexual.
4. Convert a religious fanatic.
5. Cure a crazy person.

---— ♥ ---—

GETTING OFF ON THE RIGHT FOOT: THINGS TO TELL PROSPECTIVE MATES

For the mature person who is interested in a serious relationship, it's best to get everything out in the open right up front. You already know what you want—why waste any more time than necessary finding out whether one prospective mate or another is going to fill the bill? Skip the amenities. Get straight to the point.

If you are a man:

1. Tell her you've never found a woman who could put up with you.
2. Tell her you've never found a woman who was able to sustain a relationship for more than three weeks.
3. Tell her you've learned you could never be satisfied with just one woman and, just out of curiosity, how does she feel about threesomes and open marriages?

DEVELOPING RAW MATERIAL: MAKEOVER SUGGESTIONS

REVISED ATTIRE

REVISED ATTIRE
AND PROFESSION

FIG. I: RAW FEMALE

FIG. II: RAW MALE

4. Tell her you've been married before and you wouldn't inflict that on any woman again.
5. Tell her you don't want children because you happen to know you'd make a terrible father.
6. Ask her this: If you *did* decide to have children, would she be willing to raise them in your religion instead of hers?

If you are a woman:

1. Explain that your career comes first and that you wouldn't want to get trapped in any relationship where you'd be expected to cook and clean and keep house.
2. Tell him of your time pressure to have babies.
3. Decide to have his baby without telling him.
4. Tell him he's a terrific guy and you could have some terrific times together, but you're not physically attracted to him.
5. Tell him you're willing to have a limited, superficial relationship with him, but you're very involved with this married person in Europe, and if that situation is too painful then you'd better call it quits right now.
6. Tell him you'd love to have a close personal relationship with him as long as you can keep it platonic, but you're frankly bored with men these days because

every time you find one you can really be friends with and trust, you start spending loads of time together, talking and shopping and cuddling in bed and taking showers together, and sooner or later he always gets the wrong idea and wants to have sex and ruin the whole friendship.

7. Tell him he's a real sweetheart and exactly the type of man you should fall in love with, except you always end up falling for these terrible guys who break your heart.

8. Tell him you're just getting over a very traumatic relationship with someone and you're afraid you're not going to be very good company for about two years.

––––––––––––––– ♥ –––––––––––––––

KEEPING YOUR OPTIONS OPEN
WHEN YOUR MATE WANTS
TO GET MORE SERIOUS

All right, let's say you've failed to drive your prospective mate away. As a matter of fact, this person actually seems to want to get more serious.

You may decide it's best not to let your relationship go too far. You may decide it's best to keep your options open.

Why does your lover want to get more serious with you,

anyway? Is he or she having trouble finding other dates? Don't others find this person attractive, or what? Emotionally, is he or she a bottomless pit that you're going to be expected to fill? Who can take that kind of responsibility, anyway?

If you're spending five nights a week together and your lover pressures you to make it six, that's O.K. But you'll want to keep at least one night a week open, in case you meet some-body better. If you gave up all your nights you'd feel trapped.

Imagine one day deciding to commit yourself 100 percent to your lover and then finding out the very next day that Prince Charles secretly wanted you as a replacement for Princess Diana. Or that Hugh Hefner had chosen you—providing you were still uncommitted—to take over for him as head of his sex empire. If you had kept your options open instead of committing your-self, who can guess what kind of life you might have led.

This doesn't mean you want to abandon your lover right this minute. It just means you want to be available when Prince Charles or Hugh Hefner calls you up.

VALENTINE FOR THE UNCOMMITTED

FIDELITY TEST

Under what circumstances might you be tempted to be unfaithful to your lover? Answer Yes or No to each of the following.

For Women:

1. Prince Andrew sees a snapshot of you, is overcome with love, Telexes you a proposal of marriage, and offers you a permanent place in the royal family.
   - ☐ YES
   - ☐ NO

2. A rich orthodontist in Chicago invites you on a madcap weekend in Peoria.
   - ☐ YES
   - ☐ NO

3. A moderately attractive stockboy smiles at you in the supermarket.
   - ☐ YES
   - ☐ NO

For Men:

1. Two teenaged lingerie models become hopelessly enamored of you after glimpsing you in a department store and invite you on a weekend in the South of France at their expense.
   - ☐ YES
   - ☐ NO

2. A cute waitress at Bob's Big Boy in Encino invites you to a motel in West Covina.
   - ☐ YES
   - ☐ NO

3. A female gas station attendant winks at you in a Full-Service island in Patchogue.
   - ☐ YES
   - ☐ NO

Key for Both Men and Women:

If you said Yes to #1, you are a hopeless romantic and your lover is in no danger of losing you.

If you said Yes to #1 and #2, your threshold of temptation is not exceptional.

If you said Yes to #1, #2, and #3, you are more than likely to contract herpes by the end of the year.

If you said No to all the above, your lover is reading this with you.

— ♥ —

LIVING TOGETHER
IN TWO PLACES
(Or "Why Do I Bother Keeping My Own Apartment?")

Living together in two places is the optimum situation for anyone truly desirous of avoiding love and marriage. Living together in two places is so awful that almost no one can stand it. Couples who advance to this stage of a relationship often break up just for the joy of being able to sleep in the same bed two nights in a row, or for the security of knowing that if it should rain, they're at the house that has the umbrella. (NOTE: There are a misguided few who marry, rather than break up, for the same reasons.)

GETTING YOUR FIRST DRAWER
AT YOUR LOVER'S APARTMENT

In every loving relationship there comes the memorable day when you are granted your first drawer—your first foothold—in your lover's apartment. Here you will keep things you have outgrown or previously cast away, as well as cheap imitations of all the wonderful things that are sitting unused at your own apartment. Every time you open your new drawer in your lover's apartment, take out your old razor, and nick yourself shaving, you will curse the day you met your lover and began this miserable lifestyle.

(NOTE: Once you are awarded the first drawer, your relationship will move forward at breakneck speed. Privileges like possessing a key to your lover's home or being allowed to answer his or her phone will follow immediately—usually in as little as two years.)

LIVING OUT OF A SUITCASE

There is nothing more appealing than coming home from a hard day at the office and packing up what you think you're going to want to wear to work tomorrow. Let's say you're a woman, and today was a scorchingly hot Indian summer day. You choose a cool cotton dress and open-toed shoes. Tonight you

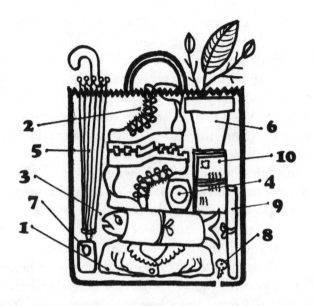

X-RAY VIEW OF TYPICAL SHOPPING BAG FOR UNMARRIED FEMALE TO TRANSPORT TO AND FROM LOVER'S APARTMENT

1. Tomorrow's dress for work, wadded up, permanently wrinkled, and appropriate for 30 degrees warmer or cooler. **2.** Hiking boots mistakenly packed for wear with dress at work. **3.** Inadequately wrapped entrée for tonight's dinner, which is leaking quietly onto dress. **4.** Empty case for diaphragm mistakenly left in own apartment. **5.** Umbrella which is never in the same apartment you wake up in on rainy days. **6.** Plant dying of malnutrition which are taking to lover's apartment in hopes of reviving. **7.** Remote beeper for answering machine which you have once again forgotten to turn on. **8.** Key to lover's apartment which took you a year to get, and which is about to slip through hole in bottom of bag. **9.** Lease for renewal on apartment you spend scarcely 30% of your time in. **10.** Last week's mail, including final notice for package to be picked up at post office, although it has already gone back to sender, and worried letter from your parents saying that they keep phoning you at all hours of the day and night and wondering where you *are*, for God's sake.

wrap them neatly in tissue paper and put them in a new shopping bag, because you have to meet a client for dinner before going to your lover's apartment and you would prefer that your client believe you're an avid shopper, not a bag lady.

The next morning at your lover's you awake to a freak snow-storm. You borrow your lover's old raincoat and trudge to work in your sundress, spend the day fielding wisecracks from your co-workers, and end up with bronchitis.

Is there anything worse than showing up at work wearing a sundress in a snowstorm? Perhaps. You could show up at a board meeting in a black silk evening dress and rhinestone earrings.

Or, let's say you meet your lover for dinner after work. It's getting late and you're both tired. Your mate says that, even though it's his or her turn to stay the night at your house, he or she has a very important business meeting early tomorrow morn-ing and begs you not to insist on going to your place. Your mate offers to spend the next two consecutive nights at your house as compensation. Being a decent person, you give in. And, since you had not planned on spending the night out, you then get to WEAR THE SAME THING TO WORK TWO DAYS IN SUCCESSION. This always makes a big hit with your boss, as well as with your rivals and detractors at the office. (NOTE: Underwear need not be a problem, since you can always get a good two days' wear out of it by turning it inside out.)

THE LAW OF THE BETTER APARTMENT

Eventually, in all living-together-in-two-places relationships, the partner with the less good apartment finds that he or she is artfully pressured into spending a greater (and therefore unequal) amount of time at the better apartment. Each day the owner of the less good apartment returns home from work, collects the mail, waters the plants, chooses the next day's wardrobe, and proceeds to the better apartment to spend the night. Then comes the sad day when the owner of the less good apartment returns home from work, collects the mail, waters the plants, and realizes that every stick of his or her clothing is at the better apartment.

What to do?

When you complain that all your clothes are at your lover's house, you'll be told that your lover could hardly help noticing the same thing. That, in fact, your clothes are expanding to fill all the available space, and that he or she no longer feels the apartment belongs to him or her.

You will then:

1. Have a screaming fight.
2. Cram ten shopping bags full of clothing.
3. Return to your modest apartment, which no longer seems like home.
4. Unpack.

5. Accept your lover's heartfelt apology over the phone.
6. Repack.
7. Return to your lover's apartment.
8. Repeat steps 1–7 as necessary.

This brings us to:

---------------------- ♥ ----------------------

GREENBURG'S LAW:
NATURE ABHORS A COUPLE
WITH SIMILAR HABITS

The chances that any two people who choose to live together will be compatible in personal habits are extremely remote. Inevitably, one person will leave socks and underwear and magazines all over the floor, while the other will be obsessed with neatness.

One will love fresh air, open windows, and a room temperature of never more than 50 degrees, while the other will insist on windows being shut tight and feel comfortable only when the room temperature is above 80.

One will feel that the only time to arise is shortly after dawn and the only time to go to bed is right after dinner, while the other can't seem to get out of bed before 11:00 a.m. nor get to bed till 2:00 or 3:00 a.m.

To every law there is a corollary.

O'MALLEY'S COROLLARY:
BUT NOT ALWAYS

In some instances, two people find, upon moving in together, that they have identical personal preferences in all areas. Should this be the case with you and your mate, *one of you will have to change.*

One of you will have to alter drastically his or her lifestyle in order to be at total odds with the other's hours, temperatures, and temperament. It doesn't matter which of you is the one to change, provided that the instant the change has been accomplished, you *begin to invest all of your energy in trying to convert your mate to your newfound lifestyle.*

Despite a total incompatibility in lifestyles—or because of it—many couples who live together still decide to take the next step and contemplate marriage.

WHEN MARRIAGE SEEMS INEVITABLE

Once you have an Intimate Romantic Relationship established, and marriage seems inevitable, you'll probably want to do one of two things:

1. Get your lover to dump you. Or:
2. Dump your lover before he or she has a chance

to dump *you*. (Make sure it looks like his or her fault, not yours.)

Generally speaking, it is easier (i.e., generates less annoying guilt) to arrange to be dumped than it is to do the dumping yourself. Popular methods of arranging to be dumped include:

1. Trying to make your lover over in the image of your ex.
2. Telling your lover that every serious relationship you've ever had has ended after precisely three months, with the other party falling passionately back in love with a former lover.
3. Demanding to spend more and more time with your lover even though you're beginning not to like him or her all that much any more. Then, when your demands are met, complaining that he or she doesn't care for you at all.
4. Making the smallest mishap into a major calamity by bursting into tears and screaming at your lover: "Now you've ruined *everything!*"
5. Letting your lover know that your relationship with him or her is in constant jeopardy. Whether this person comments on something as serious as your not telling your parents about him or her, or something as minor as your car needing a tune-up, underscore your inconstancy by replying: "This relationship is not working out."

6. Taking your lover completely for granted. Being in-attentive and insensitive and wondering what you saw in him or her in the first place.

After your lover has fled into the night, you will probably want to decide that he or she was The Real Thing after all, and that you were too blind to see it. It is common practice, at this point, to go completely to pieces and spend the rest of your life in futile attempts to arrange a reconciliation.

—————————————— ♥ ——————————————

FINDING A NEW PLACE TO LIVE AFTER BREAKING UP WITH YOUR LOVER

When you and your lover break up, one—or both—of you will move to new residences better suited to the single lifestyle. If you are the person who has left (the Leaver), you can neutralize the sympathetic advantage held by the person you have left (the Leavee) by making yourself seem far worse off than they. If you choose a miserable enough new home for yourself, you will be almost indistinguishable from the Leavee.

Regardless of whether you're the Leaver or the Leavee, you'll want to make sure that your new home is far beneath your station in life. A place that is uncomfortably small and monastic, with no charm or other redeeming features, will suit your needs perfectly. If you are the Leaver, take absolutely nothing with you to your new place. If you are the Leavee, take everything you can get your hands on, but sell or give away anything particularly good on the premise that it's too big, too elegant, too valuable or showy for your new spartan surroundings.

You won't buy any furniture or dishes, since you can always find perfectly serviceable replacements at a thrift shop or on the street before garbage pickups. You won't hang pictures on the walls, put shades over naked bulbs, or do anything at all that would make the place look homey. You won't under any circumstances unpack your cartons of belongings (with the exception of the carton containing depressing books by French Existentialist authors). This way, there will never be any doubt in your mind that this move is only a temporary measure.

If, within thirty years, your mate has not come back to reclaim you, you can permit yourself to unpack the cartons or move to a nicer place, whichever you prefer.

IMPORTANT NOTE: Even if you were the one who left, you could still wait for your mate to reclaim you. You know that if your mate had really loved you he or she would never have let you leave.

PHILOSOPHICAL LOVE TEST

Ask your beloved the following question: "If we were on a plane and it crashed, would you prefer that we *both* died, or just me?"

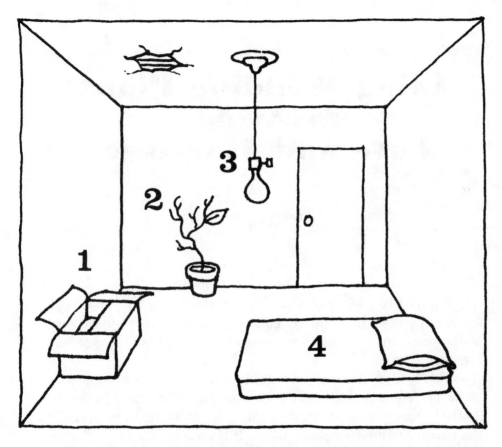

IDEAL DECORATING SCHEME FOR APARTMENT TO LIVE IN
AFTER BREAKING UP WITH YOUR LOVER

1. Unpacked carton of books, magazines and records too evocative of painful memories to be unpacked. **2.** Dying plant with one surviving leaf—a last remnant of a dead relationship. **3.** Bare bulb—all you really need to see, unless you're up to choosing some kind of lampshade or other fixture, which is such a commitment. **4.** Spartan mattress on the floor—who needs bed frames and box springs and all that kind of junk, especially since who knows how long you're even going to be there.

Using Wedding Plans to Avoid Love and Marriage

COMMITMENT

Everybody who ever gives advice about love and marriage stresses the need for commitment. Commitment, they say, is one of the most crucial ingredients in any relationship as serious as marriage.

This is utter nonsense. What kind of word is "commitment," anyway? "He was *committed* to an institution for the criminally insane." "She was *committed* to the federal penitentiary because she had *committed* manslaughter." Right away you know "commitment" is not a fun word. Why would men and women want to *commit* themselves to anything? And what's more, why should they have to?

— ♥ —
QUIZ

Choose the fun word from each of the following pairs of words:

1. Petting / Commitment
2. French kissing / Commitment
3. One-night-stand / Commitment
4. Cheap thrills / Commitment
5. Walking the dog / Commitment

———————— ♥ ————————

VALID REASONS TO GET MARRIED

Some cynical people believe there are no valid reasons for getting married, but this position is absolutely untenable. There *are* circumstances under which getting married is advisable. Here are some valid reasons* to get married:

1. Trying to prove something or other.
2. Meeting somebody new and spending a nice night with him or her.
3. Trying to punish a former lover who rejected you.
4. Trying to punish a parent by marrying somebody of a different religion or a different race or the same sex.

* Note that pregnancy is no longer a valid reason to get married.

THINGS TO CONSIDER BEFORE
COMMITTING YOURSELF TO SOMETHING
AS SERIOUS AS MARRIAGE

All right, let's say your reason to get married *is* one of the foregoing. Before proceeding any further, ask yourself the following:

1. What if I meet somebody cuter?
2. Which one of us is going to die first?
3. Which one of us would I *prefer* died first?
4. What is this person going to look like in thirty or forty years?
5. Why commit myself to somebody who in thirty or forty years might get sick or ugly or die?
6. Why would I want to share a bathroom?

HOW TO OBTAIN MAXIMUM
GRIEF FROM WEDDING PLANS

You have repressed all your fears and are proceeding with the wedding plans. Fine, if that's what you really want to do.

It is devoutly to be hoped that you have insisted on paying for your own wedding—that way it will be completely yours and not your parents'. It is further hoped that you've decided on a big wedding, sparing no expense. Starting a marriage in crushing debt builds character, assuming you survive.

On the other hand, why not begin married life with your *parents* in crushing debt instead of you? Don't worry about the financial hardship your parents will be forced to endure just so you can be happy on your wedding day. A parent's financial participation in a child's wedding in no way increases the amount of pressure placed on the child to have a successful marriage (how could your parents possibly exert any *more* pressure?).

An added benefit of the parent-sponsored wedding is that you will be spared the fatiguing duties of planning the event. Mom and Dad will take care of everything—from the wedding attire to the guest list: What groom wouldn't love a brown brocade tuxedo, and what better time than your wedding to meet your mother's cousin's hairdresser's sister? Imagine your names on the marquee outside the Holiday Inn, the contemporary beat of the Homer Gomez Trio, a lovely sliced brisket of beef, maybe some little pigs in blankets, and a cash bar. Nice.

If you've been wise enough to select somebody of a faith other than your own as a marriage partner, you will probably decide—even if neither of you practices his religion—to make both religions part of the ceremony. Try to find priests or rabbis or imams who will officiate in tandem.

The pleasure of your company
is requested at the
almost definite marriage of
Suzanne O'Malley & Dan Greenburg
on, say
Saturday the twenty-eighth of June
around a quarter past seven o'clock at
The Lotos Club
5 East 66th Street in New York
or
some other time and place
but probably to each other
although not necessarily

R.S.V.P.   Black tie requested
                but call to make sure

WEDDING INVITATION FOR THE UNCOMMITTED

KEEPING YOUR OPTIONS OPEN
AFTER YOU HAVE ACCEPTED
A PROPOSAL OF MARRIAGE

It is never too late to back out of a plan to get married. Don't allow considerations about money to force you to go ahead with a marriage you don't want. Even after spending $500 on engraved wedding invitations, you can simply decide not to send them out. A $500 investment down the drain is *nothing* compared to the alternative of ruining the rest of your life. You can always tear the printed portion of the invitation off and use the blank part and the envelopes for personal stationery. And with a little imagination—like taking up the hem and cutting off the seed pearls—even a non-returnable bridal gown can be transformed into a practical dress for home or office.

BACKING OUT ON THE
DAY OF THE WEDDING

Just because a hundred relatives are coming in from rural towns in Kansas and Texas doesn't mean you have to go through with the wedding. Your relatives have probably wanted to see you for a long time anyway, and will be pleased just to have a family reunion. The gifts they brought with them can either be returned or kept by means of a little joke, like: "I'll just hang onto this darling little ceramic bagel dish and then you won't have to send me a present next Christmas."

Backing out of marriage on the day of your wedding is the greatest opportunity to avoid entanglement of all. Except for one:

---------------- ♥ ----------------

BACKING OUT DURING
THE ACTUAL CEREMONY

Do not fall under the popular misconception that backing out during the actual ceremony is a failure, a cop-out, or something of which to be ashamed. When the clergyperson says: "Do you take this man (or woman) to be your lawfully wedded husband (or wife)?" is the ideal time to seriously address yourself to this question.

You probably think that "Yes" or "No" are the only possible responses, but this is only due to shortsightedness on your part. The following are just a few of the

Possible Responses to the Question
"Do You Take This Man (or Woman)
to be Your Lawfully Wedded Spouse?"

While the clergyperson is waiting for your answer, turn around and scan the wedding party. See if there might be anybody else who'd suit you better as a mate. If you see anybody cute whom you'd like to date, simply turn back to the clergyperson and say: "I think not."

If you're uncertain what to answer the clergyperson and need a little more time to think about it, say: "Can I get back to you on that?"

If you're the bride, take this moment to consider how sexist it is for the woman to have to commit herself first. Why should a woman have to say "Yes" first and leave herself open to a possible rejection if the groom decides to back out? You might reply instead: "Why don't you ask *him* first? Why do *I* always have to be the one to make decisions?"

Or you can make a conditional response: "I will if *he* will."

♥

THE WEDDING RECEPTION

Let's say you've both answered the clergyperson's question affirmatively. You can take your mind off the enormity of what you've just committed yourself to by focusing on something extraneous. Like the expense of the wedding reception.

Walk around and subtly remind everybody who is eating anything what it cost you: "How do you like that four-dollar hors d'oeuvre you're eating?" Or: "Hey, you probably don't spend seventy-five dollars apiece when you go out to a restaurant, but that's what it's costing us to feed you tonight."

Just pray that you can make back most of the cost of food and liquor from their wedding gifts.

A MESSAGE TO THE
INEXPERIENCED BRIDE ABOUT SEX

Now that the wedding reception is over, here are some helpful thoughts for the anxious bride to contemplate on the most important occasion of her life, the Wedding Night:

Remember how your Mom and Dad and clergyperson and teachers always told you when you were a little girl and when you were growing up how sexual relations between a man and a woman were filthy and dirty and disgusting and demeaning and immoral and a sin against God? Well, starting tonight, your wedding night, they're not.

Sexual relations between a husband and wife are *not* the same as sexual relations between a man and a woman. Sexual relations between a husband and wife are perfectly acceptable. And clean. Sexual relations between a husband and wife may *look* and *feel* and *sound* and *smell* filthy and dirty and disgusting and demeaning and immoral and a sin against God, but they're not.

WHAT TO DO ON
YOUR WEDDING NIGHT

If you've never had sex together before, your wedding night is the perfect time to get to know each other intimately. After the physical and emotional exhaustion of the wedding, and your departure from the bosom of your families, you will finally find yourselves completely alone in a strange hotel, preferably in a foreign country, a country in which you can neither speak the language nor drink the water without getting diarrhea, a country in which, ideally, there has been recent political unrest.

Even if you and your betrothed have been sleeping together for years, the wedding night is an occasion of powerful significance. You probably have a rigid picture of what the event should be like. You probably expect that your lovemaking will be perfect, lyrical, memorable, and a test of whether or not you should remain together.

Insist on having champagne in your room, even if you're already drunk. Don't worry about pregnancy or disease or bedbugs or deadly foreign vermin or impotence. Especially don't worry about impotence.

Don't even think about the Baltimore man who, although he'd been making love successfully to his fiancée for five months before the wedding, failed to get it up on his wedding night. Or, for that matter, ever again.

You can both expect to have thrilling and simultaneous climaxes—even if you've never had an orgasm before. Just before you begin the act, take your mate's hand and say: "Just think, honey, whatever we do in the next hour we'll remember for the rest of our lives."

THE REST OF THE HONEYMOON

Try not to think about your post-nuptial depression or what happened on your wedding night. Never speak of it to your mate or to anybody else. If you don't acknowledge it, maybe it will eventually cease to have happened.

Try not to think about your hangover or about how horrible you feel. Think about the new apartment you have rented and how much more it cost than you could afford and what it's costing you right now while it stands idle and unused.

Figure out exactly what you're paying by the hour in this suffocatingly disappointing hotel and keep mentioning the figure to your mate.

Try to get all your sunbathing in on the first day, between dashes to the toilet, and don't bother putting on suntan lotion because you were at the beach a month ago and you probably still have a good base. (Should you learn that your base wasn't as good as you thought it was, you'll be able to spend the next three days in a bathtub full of ice cubes and then begin peeling dead skin off your body in foot-long strips.)

Daily Life, or:
The Honeymoon
Is Over

♥

DAILY MARITAL LIFE

Now that the honeymoon is over, you're going to have a little time to kill together. Like the rest of your lives. What are you planning to do with all that time? Aren't you afraid you'll run out of small talk? Wouldn't it be awful if you had to spend forty or fifty years in each other's company and you completely ran out of things to chat about after six months?

Well, fortunately for you, our next section deals with such things: adding spice to daily marital life, entertaining your mate by mimicking what he or she says, what to do if either you or your mate gets sick, proper attitude toward parents and in-laws, proper behavior for driving with your mate, how to help your mate tell a funny story, how to ruin sleeping together without even having sex, and much much more.

And now, on to our first lesson in daily marital living.

EXCUSE ME COULD YOU PLEASE SAY THAT AGAIN I DON'T BELIEVE I HEARD YOU CORRECTLY LISTEN JUST WHO THE HELL DO YOU THINK YOU ARE FOR GOD'S SAKE WHAT AM I SUPPOSED TO BE YOUR SERVANT DON'T YOU DARE TALK TO ME IN THAT TONE OF VOICE I GUESS WE JUST AREN'T MEANT TO BE TOGETHER THAT'S ALL I'VE HAD IT UP TO HERE WITH YOU THAT'S RIGHT YOU HEARD ME THAT'S NOT MEANT TO BE A THREAT WE'RE JUST IN DIFFERENT TIMES IN OUR LIFE O.K. GO AHEAD THEN LEAVE I'LL HELP YOU PACK YOUR BAGS I GUESS WE DON'T NEED TO BE TOGETHER OH THAT'S CUTE REAL CUTE I DON'T HAVE TO STAND HERE AND TAKE THAT FROM YOU YOU KNOW WHERE ARE YOU GOING THAT'S A LAUGH I CAN'T BELIEVE YOU SAID THAT I CAN'T BELIEVE YOU COULD ACTUALLY SAY SUCH A THING TO ME THAT'S THE THANKS I GET THAT'S PROBABLY JUST WHAT I DESERVE FOR PUTTING UP WITH YOU ALL THESE YEARS I RUE THE DAY I MET YOU YOU'RE NOT AT ALL SUPPORTIVE OF MY LIFE OR OUR RELATIONSHIP OR ANYTHING ELSE WHY DO I WASTE MY TIME WHY DO I WASTE MY BREATH THIS IS THE LAST STRAW I DON'T KNOW WHAT YOU'RE GETTING OUT OF THIS WHAT'S THE PSYCHIC PAYOFF IN ALL THIS FOR YOU I MEAN WHAT IS ALL THIS REALLY ABOUT YOU KNOW WHAT YOU ARE YOU'RE SICK THAT'S WHAT YOU ARE YOU NEED A GODDAM PSYCHIATRIST I HAVE A GOOD MIND TO PICK UP THE PHONE AND TELL YOUR MOTHER EXACTLY WHAT YOU SAID THAT'S RIGHT TURN AWAY FROM ME YOU HAVEN'T HEARD A SINGLE WORD I'VE SAID ALL EVENING WHY CAN'T YOU FIGHT LIKE A MAN WHAT'S THAT SUPPOSED TO MEAN THAT I'M NOT A MAN DO YOU THINK YOU COULD REPEAT THAT IN ENGLISH WHAT AM I SUPPOSED TO BE A MINDREADER OR WHAT YOU DON'T HAVE THE GUTS TO LEAVE ME OH NO WELL WE'LL JUST SEE ABOUT THAT LEAVE ME ALONE JUST LEAVE ME ALONE HEY WHERE ARE YOU GOING I'M LEAVING YOU ALONE COME BACK HERE THIS INSTANT NO IT'S TOO LATE IT'S OVER IF YOU WALK THROUGH THAT DOOR DON'T EVER BOTHER COMING BACK HERE AGAIN FINE THAT'S JUST FINE WITH ME YOU'RE GOING TO BE VERY SORRY YOU SAID THAT OH REALLY SAY THAT AGAIN I DARE YOU WHAT'S THE MATTER ARE YOU DEAF YOU DON'T DESERVE SOMEBODY AS GOOD AS ME WE MIGHT JUST AS WELL END IT RIGHT NOW I'M SERIOUS I'VE HAD IT UP TO HERE WITH YOU

WALLPAPER DESIGN FOR THE MARITAL BEDROOM

ADDING SPICE TO
DAILY MARITAL LIFE

Let's face it, living with somebody, no matter how wonderful you thought he or she was initially, is boring. Doing the same old things, day after day, saying the same old things in the same old way—what can you do to liven things up?

Well, one thing you can do is to flavor communiqués to your mate with wit, humor, irony—and yes, even sarcasm. Wit, humor, irony—and yes, even sarcasm—are to a bland conversation what MSG is to food. How dull it is to ask for the salt, day after day, by saying: "Would you please pass me the salt?" How much more interesting it is to rephrase it thus: *"Would it be too much to ask for you to pass me the salt?"*

Get the idea?

WORDS OF ENDEARMENT

As a married person, you will learn a new use for tender words of endearment like "honey," "sweetheart," or "darling." Married people's use of such words is far different from that of single people. For example:

1. *"Honey,* would you take out the garbage?"
2. *"Sweetheart,* do you *have* to smoke at the table?"
3. *"Pussycat,* please don't touch me there."

4. *"Darling,* it's your turn to go out for the Sunday paper."

5. *"My angel,* could you find the plunger and unplug the toilet?"

———— ♥ ————

MIMICKING

One of the most effective and entertaining techniques you can use in Daily Marital Life is Mimicking. In order to master this subtle art, you will have to learn The Basic Facial Expression, The Basic Stance, and The Basic Tone of Voice.

The Basic Facial Expression: Stand in front of a mirror. Imagine you are sucking a lemon. Watch how your mouth shrivels up, your upper lip almost touches your nose, your nostrils enlarge, your eyes scroonch up, and your brow becomes furrowed, all at once. Imagine you are cleaning up a BM that your puppy made on the living-room carpet. This is The Basic Facial Expression.

The Basic Stance: Place your hands on your hips, tilt your head to one side, thrust your torso forward and your buttocks back like Mick Jagger, shaking your head and shoulders from side to side. This is The Basic Stance.

The Basic Tone of Voice: Pitch your voice two octaves above that of your mate, accenting and drawing out every second or third syllable. This is The Basic Tone of Voice.

What to Mimic: Mimic anything your mate says that is particularly fatuous, self-important, or self-pitying. You can mimic statements like: "You know, you're really immature," or "You are never to use that woman's name in my house."

Let's say your mate has just made a statement like, "I forbid you to talk to me in that tone of voice." Adopt The Basic Facial Expression, The Basic Stance, and The Basic Tone of Voice, and say: "I for-*bid* you to *tawwwk* to me in that *tone* of *voiiiccce!*" Go ahead. Give it a try.

❤

IN SICKNESS AND IN HEALTH

At various times during even the shortest of marriages, one mate or the other will get sick. It is important to know how to behave in such situations in order to milk from them as much resentment and pathos as possible. The following are intended as general guidelines to sick behavior:

1. *What to do if your mate gets sick:* Be very solicitous for the first two hours. Insist that your mate get into bed, and take his or her temperature. Offer to make breakfast and bring it to your mate on a tray, but then forget and cause your mate to remind you repeatedly to do what you offered until you can get justifiably irritated at what you perceive as nagging. Then stomp into the kitchen, throw various utensils noisily around, stalk back to the bedroom, and serve the meal, bristling with resentment, and belittling the severity of your mate's affliction.

2. *What to do if* YOU *get sick:* Suffer as audibly as possible. Exaggerate all your symptoms—if you have a mild sore throat, pretend you can't speak at all. If you have a slight cough, wheeze and choke and gag and try to bring up a little blood. If you have a cold, pretend it's the flu. If you have the flu, pretend it's pneumonia. If you have a mild stomach ailment, pretend it's Something Worse. (There are various techniques for heating up a thermometer to make it read 105 degrees that all schoolchildren know, and which we needn't go into here.)

Complain that your mate is ignoring you, that you take much better care of him or her when the situation is reversed (a bold-faced lie). Ask your mate to do absolutely everything for you, especially things you can do yourself.

If all of the above doesn't work, Get Sicker. (See Sickness as Punishment on p. 120.)

3. *What to do if you're both well:* Become a health food and exercise nut. Do an hour's worth of calisthenics every day in your bedroom before arising and before retiring—preferably while your mate is trying to sleep. Inhale and exhale extra noisily. Jounce about on the bed.

Insist your mate start dieting, stop drinking and smoking. If he or she is already dieting or is trying to give up drinking or smoking, put more energy into your mate's program than your mate.

Pop at least a dozen vitamins at every meal. Announce you are cutting out all unhealthy foods from your diet. Refuse to have the following in your home: lamb, ham, pork, bacon, steaks, hamburgers, shrimp, lobster, veal, eggs, white bread, white flour, white rice, sugar, salt, caffeinated coffee, decaffeinated coffee, caffeinated tea, decaffeinated tea, cake, cookies, ice cream, all canned foods, and anything made with preservatives.

Bring into your home healthy foods like bean sprouts, alfalfa sprouts, seaweed, kale, wheat germ, yeast, honey, goat's milk, unsweetened yogurt, tofu, dried fruit, and various meat-substitute foods cunningly made from soy beans. Read aloud the ingredients on the label of anything your mate brings home, and sneer. If your mate suggests you eat any substance you believe to be unhealthy, stare in shock and say: "So, you're really trying to kill me, aren't you!"

♥
PROPER ATTITUDE TOWARD
PARENTS AND IN-LAWS

A vital part of Daily Marital Life is taken up with parents and in-laws. Here are some basic guidelines for the Proper Attitude Toward Parents and In-Laws:

1. How to treat your mate's parents if your mate adores them: Accuse your mate of being unhealthily tied to them. Point out any of their shortcomings that your mate might have missed. Mention these shortcomings often. Complain whenever plans to get together with your in-laws are contemplated and arrange to have prior commitments.

2. How to treat your mate's parents if your mate can't stand them: Accuse your mate of being childishly rebellious, disrespectful, and ungrateful. Extol your in-laws' virtues, even if you have to totally make them up. Complain that you don't get together with them enough and invite them to your house for weekends as a surprise to your mate. Flirt with the parent of the opposite sex. Always put your arms around them and call them Mom and Dad.

3. How to deal with your own parents where your mate is concerned: Feel free to criticize your parents unmercifully, but when your mate does so, leap to their defense and reminisce about how generous they've been to your mate on birthdays and Christmas. If you employ this stratagem enough, your mate will eventually catch on and refuse to say anything but complimentary things about your parents. Your countermove to this is to say: "Why is it that you *consistently* take their side against me?"

PROPER ATTITUDE TOWARD YOUR FRIENDS VS. YOUR MATE'S FRIENDS

The rules for parents and in-laws may be applied to Your Friends vs. Your Mate's Friends.

PROPER BEHAVIOR FOR DRIVING WITH MATE

Daily Marital Life includes numerous social and business engagements outside the home, which you will have to attend as a couple.

Arrange to have your mate take down detailed directions to any destination you have to drive to together. While en route, make every effort to dispute your mate's interpretation of these directions. Get thoroughly lost and blame your mate for your predicament. (NOTE: See Sample Directions Mate Took on Cocktail Napkin to Get to Important Party in Suburbs on p. 47.)

Do not criticize your mate's driving ability. Do sit in the passenger's seat next to your mate and practice wincing, uttering barely audible gasps and sharp intakes of breath at critical moments, coupled with stepping on an imaginary brake pedal on the floor in front of you. Do offer helpful driving tips:

1. "Honey, I *think* your blinker is still on."
2. "You know, I just read somewhere that gas consumption in our model of car is much more efficient at 55 m.p.h. than at 90 m.p.h."
3. "Sweetheart, is it possible your brights are on?"
4. "Gee, I notice it's starting to rain. Maybe you'd like to turn on the windshield wipers."

♥

HOW TO HELP YOUR MATE
TELL A FUNNY STORY

At a dinner party of friends or business associates, suggest that your mate regale the assembled guests with an account of an amusing experience that the two of you have shared. For maximum amusement value, assist your mate in the regaling. The following suggestions will be of immeasurable help:

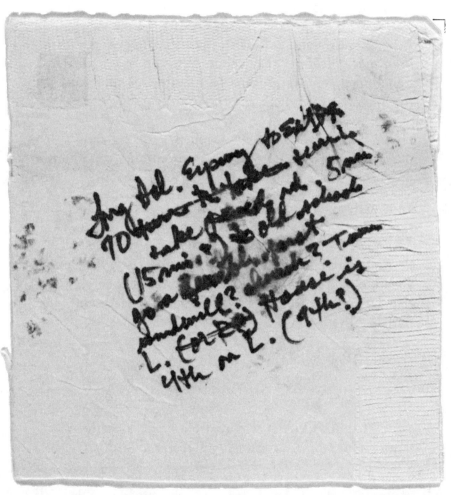

Sample Directions Mate Took on Cocktail Napkin to Get to Important
Dinner Party in Suburbs.

1. Beg your mate to tell the story in his or her own inimitable fashion. An anecdote in which your mate does something inept and ultimately dangerous only adds to the fun.

YOU: "Honey, why don't you tell the folks about that hilarious time we were in Mexico and you almost drove our car off the cliff?"

Your mate will chuckle good-naturedly and begin telling the story. As soon as this happens, you should:

2. Start correcting every detail of the story. Providing accurate details will mean the difference between a story that has people rolling on the floor with mirth and one that has them wearing polite, strained smiles.

MATE: "Well, when we were in Acapulco last February, we rented a little Jeep, and the roads were so bad that——"

YOU: "I don't think it was really a *Jeep*, sweetheart, it was a Brazilian *knockoff* of a Jeep called a Gurgel."

MATE: "Well, whatever, we were driving down this narrow——"

you: "Also, I don't think it was Acapulco. I think the thing that happened in Acapulco was that you lost control of the car in the marketplace and you drove over that man's pottery and he got so mad he called the police. The time you drove off the *cliff* was in Cozumel."

3. Interrupt your mate whenever necessary to fill in parts of the story that he or she left out.

mate: "Well, anyway, wherever the damned thing happened, there we were in this Jeep—or this Jeep knockoff, whatever they called it—and the road we were driving on was only one lane, and it had so many hairpin curves that we—"

you: "You know, I really think you have to tell them that just before we started driving, we'd been drinking at this little Mexican café, and we were already a little smashed. Also, by then it was dark out, and our headlights were barely working. And we didn't have any pesos—that will become an important part of the story later on, as you'll see. O.K., go ahead, dear."

4. As soon as your mate has finished the story, retell it yourself the way you remember it happening.

VARIOUS SOURCES OF INFORMATION AND YOUR MATE'S ESTIMATION OF THEIR CREDIBILITY

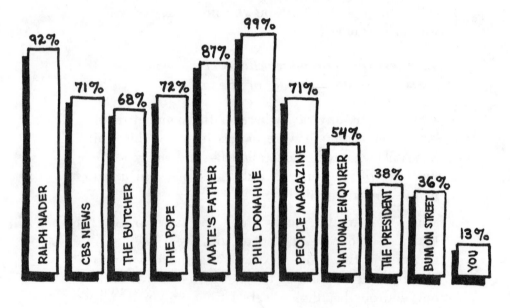

HOW TO RUIN SLEEPING TOGETHER
WITHOUT EVEN HAVING SEX

And, remember, no day in your marital life is complete without bedtime.

Here are a few ways to irritate the person you sleep with:

1. Bring little snacks to bed and lose them under the covers.
2. Complain that you want to go to sleep when he or she is in the middle of reading a really good novel or watching a really exciting program on TV.
3. If your mate is sleepy, insist on watching the *Late Late Show* right through to the bitter end, right through the credits for make-up and wardrobe and key grip and best boy, and then get hooked on the Inspirational Message and the National Anthem.
4. Begin a heated bedtime discussion with your mate, and when he or she is roused to a fever pitch, fall asleep.
5. Urge your mate to climb out of bed and intercept the robbers on the roof.
6. Sleep with your eyes partly open and roll them around in their sockets.
7. Keep tossing and turning over and over until all the

sheets and blankets are wound around you like a gyroscope and your mate is shivering in the cold.

8. Whenever you have a bad dream, growl and shriek fiercely in your sleep.

9. Fart.

Using Sex to Avoid Love in Marriage

EXCUSING YOURSELF FROM CONJUGAL DUTIES

One thing you will have to confront on a daily basis is the obligation of having marital sex. Your mate, who is probably no more anxious than you are to engage in this tedious activity, will nonetheless require you to participate, unless you present a suitable excuse.

Here are a number of approved excuses for not having sex:

1. I have a headache.
2. I have the trots.
3. I am sick to my stomach.
4. I am too congested.
5. I am too hyper.
6. I am too worried.
7. I am ovulating.

8. I am too busy now.
9. I am starting my period.
10. I am saving my strength for the big game.
11. I am mad at you for what you did, for what you did not do, for what you said, for what you did not say, for what you would have said, and for what you will have said next time we speak.
12. I have to work.
13. I will get pregnant.
14. It is too early.
15. I am pregnant.
16. It is too late.
17. I do not want to get all sweaty.
18. I do not want to mess up my hair.
19. I have got a yeast infection.
20. I have a case of jock itch.
21. The kids will hear.
22. We did it just the other night.
23. He has never heard of foreplay.
24. She lies there like a lox.
25. He finishes too soon.
26. It takes her too long to finish.
27. I just do not want to—I do not have to have a reason.

FIVE BONUS REASONS FOR
HUSBANDS NOT TO HAVE SEX

1. She always wants me to take long, hot bubble baths with her by candlelight, which is boring.
2. She always wants me to make love in the wilderness, which is boring.
3. She always wants me to make love without having a drink first, which is boring.
4. She always wants me to make love without pulling the shades and the curtains and locking the bedroom door, which is boring.
5. She never wants to do anything exciting or different.

FIVE BONUS REASONS FOR
WIVES NOT TO HAVE SEX

1. He always wants me to wear a garter belt and stockings, which is sick.
2. He always wants me to dress up like a nurse, which is sick.
3. He always wants me to pose for dirty Polaroid pictures, which is sick.
4. He is always trying to get me to have a threesome with another woman, which is sick.
5. He is never spontaneous, imaginative, or inventive.

27 APPROVED REASONS FOR NOT HAVING SEX WITH YOUR MATE TONIGHT, SET TO GREGORIAN CHANT

HOW TO RUIN SEX BY STAYING IN THE BATHROOM TOO LONG WHILE GETTING READY FOR BED

The longer you take in there, the better your chances that your partner will get tired of waiting for you. Many husbands and wives complain that, the bathroom being a relatively small room, they are unable to find things to do in there to occupy them for the hour or more it usually takes for their mates to become furious or fall asleep.

This is rubbish. After you have washed your face, brushed your teeth, taken your vitamins, applied moisturizing lotion to your face and hands and body, given yourself a little sponge bath, applied deodorant and cologne, ask yourself the following questions:

1. Shouldn't I clip the hairs in my nostrils?
2. Shouldn't I clip my toenails?
3. Shouldn't I pluck my eyebrows?
4. Shouldn't I squeeze that unsightly blemish?
5. Shouldn't I wax my legs or underarms?
6. Is my bald spot getting bigger and shouldn't I position two mirrors to check it out?
7. Aren't the nonslip strips in the bottom of the bathtub beginning to lose their adhesive and curl up at

the ends and shouldn't I re-glue them before they become dangerous and trip somebody?

8. Aren't the bottles in the medicine cabinet poorly arranged and shouldn't I rearrange them so that somebody who really needed medication in an emergency could find it before they bled to death?

Congratulations—your mate just fell asleep.

♥

MORE WAYS OF RUINING SEX

There are so many excellent ways to ruin the sex act that there is only room here to discuss the most obvious ones:

1. Invite sex play so unappealingly that it will turn your partner off. Here are three sample ways of phrasing your invitations: (a) "I have to be up early for work tomorrow, but I have about five minutes before I have to be asleep—is that enough time for you?" (b) "I have a stomach ache and I'm so nervous I could puke, but if you're really horny, go ahead and get it over with." (c) "I have this yucky rash, which is probably only a yeast infection and not herpes—would you like to do it, or are you too grossed out?"

2. Start foreplay at an inappropriate time. For example, grab your mate in a sexual embrace just before leaving the house to catch a plane you're already somewhat late for, or just before your mate's parents are due to arrive for dinner.

3. Start foreplay in an inappropriate place. Choose a location that is not inherently conducive to a relaxed sexual experience, like a public restroom, a city bus, or a revolving door.

4. Start foreplay at an inappropriate time AND place. Like on an elevator two floors from your destination.

5. Eliminate foreplay altogether. Foreplay is, after all, only a waste of time. Why not simply announce your intentions by roughly grabbing your mate by the genitals?

6. Indicate that whatever your mate does to you in bed is inept. He or she will appreciate the tip.

7. Make sex into a duty. Adopt one of the following approved attitudes: (a) I *ought* to have sex if I really love him/her; (b) I *ought* to have sex if I'm a real man/woman; (c) I *ought* to have sex if I'm at all normal.

8. Make yourself sexually unattractive to your partner. Stop showering or shaving on a daily basis. Put on excess weight. Slop around the house in an old terry cloth bathrobe with gravy stains. Emit noises and smells not generally applauded in public.

9. Make a great session of lovemaking into a cause for resentment. Great sex is very threatening. You could get used to it, and then you might become even more vulnerable to, and dependent upon, your mate. If he or she left you, it would destroy you. No, far better to pull away. Dismiss that great session of lovemaking you had as a fluke. Or better yet, use it as the standard by which all future lovemaking must be measured. Best of all, say that you now see how good your sex together *could* have been in the past, and accuse your mate of not having had the interest to make it so, because of lack of love for you.

10. *Make your wife into your Mom or your husband into your Dad.* Most folks don't want to have sex with their Moms or Dads.

Which brings up an interesting point:

— ❤ —

HOW THE INCEST TABOO CAN WORK FOR YOU

When you were growing up in your parents' home, you were taught that it was wrong to have sexual feelings about anyone you lived with or anyone in your family. So now you're married, what makes you think the rules have changed? Your husband or wife is both someone you live with and a member of your family—how could it be any more right for you to have sexual feelings about them than it was to have them about your mother or father or sister or brother?

The answer is that it couldn't. You can expect the same terrible consequences from having sex with your spouse as with any other member of your family—it's still incest.

Now, the question is, how long can you avoid sex with somebody you not only live with but whom you sleep with in the same bed and who is always putting on sexy underwear?

SEXUAL APTITUDE TEST FOR MEN

Choose the word which does not belong:

1. Mom
2. Sister
3. Wife
4. Virgin Mary
5. Fiancée
6. Fellatio

HOW TO USE THE DIAPHRAGM

And now a word about contraception.

Most forms of contraception take the spontaneity out of sex and make it premeditated. Most people are not eager to take responsibility for premeditated sex—accidental sex is human, premeditated sex is so dirty that people try to make it tedious in reparation. The most tedious form of contraception is the diaphragm.

Which partner takes responsibility for inserting the diaphragm isn't important—either one can take the initiative for ruining the act. For example:

The male may choose to insert the diaphragm as a natural

part of loveplay. This is a splendid opportunity (1) to put it in upside down and have to take it out and do it all over again, (2) to lose it in there and have to go poking about with a flashlight, (3) to grasp it too loosely, causing it to pop out of your hand and fly across the room.

The female may, to improve spontaneity, insert the diaphragm herself prior to coming to bed. Before doing so she should say to her mate: "Listen, do you think you're going to be in the mood tonight or not? I don't see the point in putting it in if you're not." Alternatively, the female may simply insert the diaphragm *without* querying her mate, then take the subject up in bed: "Look, I don't know if you're in the mood or not, but after all the trouble I went through to put this thing inside me, the least you could do is pretend to be interested."

Should neither partner choose to initiate the sex act by inserting the diaphragm, it is almost as much fun to go fumbling about for it in the dark just prior to ejaculation.

Many gynecologists warn that the diaphragm must actually be in place in order to be effective. This is utter nonsense. Statistics show that *it is the average number of times you use the diaphragm* that counts, so the chances are that it will work for you equally well in the bureau drawer.

Besides, it's probably safe tonight anyway.

A DO-IT-YOURSELF TEST
ON SEXUAL PERFORMANCE:

Here is a little test to see how well you're doing:

1. Do you and your mate make love:
   - (a) More than once a day?
   - (b) More than once a week?
   - (c) More than once a month?
   - (d) At least once a year, whether you feel like it or not?
2. Is your relationship in bed with your mate:
   - (a) As good as it was the week you met?
   - (b) As good as that of your best friends?
   - (c) As good as the ones you see in the movies?
3. How often do you achieve orgasm?
   - (a) Every time you and your mate make love.
   - (b) Most every time you and your mate make love.
   - (c) Depends on whom you fantasize about.
   - (d) What's an orgasm?
4. Which of the following celebrities does your mate's lovemaking technique most closely resemble?
   - (a) Catherine Deneuve
   - (b) Warren Beatty
   - (c) Fred Flintstone

THE CONDOM:
SWELL, IF IT DOESN'T GROSS YOU OUT ESTHETICALLY, AND IF YOU DON'T LET IT GET ALL DRIED UP AND CRUMBLY IN YOUR WALLET, AND IF YOU DON'T WORRY ABOUT THE PINHOLES THAT CROP UP EVEN IN NEW ONES.

THE PILL:
GREAT, WITH A FEW MINOR SIDE EFFECTS, LIKE FAT, LIVER SPOTS, STRETCH MARKS, PUKING, FACIAL HAIR, AND MAYBE A TEENSY BIT OF CANCER.

THE FOAM:
EXCELLENT, PROVIDED YOU REMEMBER TO RE-APPLY IT EVERY THREE MINUTES OR SO.

THE DIAPHRAGM:
TERRIFIC, UNLESS YOU GRIP IT WRONG WHILE INSERTING AND IT SPRINGS ACROSS THE ROOM. OR UNLESS YOU CAN'T TELL THE DIFFERENCE IN THE DARK BETWEEN SPERMICIDAL CREME AND TOOTHPASTE.

THE COIL:
WELL, YOU CAN'T INSTALL IT YOURSELF —A DOCTOR HAS TO DO THAT AND IT'S KIND OF PAINFUL. THEN THERE ARE THE CRAMPS. AND THEN THERE'S ALWAYS THE DANGER OF IT PERFORATING YOUR UTERUS. AND IT DOESN'T ALWAYS PREVENT BABIES EITHER. BUT HEY, WOULDN'T IT MAKE GREAT FETUS NOSE GLASSES?

SAF-T-COIL I.U.D.   NOSE GLASSES

THE RHYTHM METHOD

M	T	W	Th	F	S	Sn	M	T	W	Th	F	S	Sn	M	T	W	Th	F	S	Sn	M	T	W	Th	F	S	Sn
1	2	3	4	5	6	7	8	9	10	11	12	13	14	15	16	17	18	19	20	21	22	23	24	25	26	27	28

| SORT OF SAFE | SORT OF UNSAFE | EVEN LESS SAFE THAN BEFORE | DEFINITELY NOT SAFE, FERTILE AS ANYTHING | MIGHT BE SAFE, AND THEN AGAIN, MIGHT NOT | GIVE IT A SHOT, WHAT THE HELL |

SOME RELIABLE, SPONTANEOUS AND CAREFREE METHODS
OF BIRTH CONTROL

♥

FAKING ORGASMS

We speak here about the faking of the female rather than the male orgasm. The faking of male orgasms is merely a sophisticated physiological tour de force and need not concern us.

Traditionally, the faking of female orgasms has been popular for two reasons: (1) It allowed the male partner to feel that he was a far better lover than he actually was; (2) it allowed the female to build up powerful and satisfying resentments.

Nowadays, women are faking orgasms less and less. Partly due to the influence of the feminist movement, and partly—and this is what is germane to our interests here—because it enables the female to accuse her partner of failing to satisfy her.

This situation is gravid with possibilities for inflicting serious damage to the male ego. Just what you are able to improvise yourself will depend upon how serious you are about wanting to ruin your marriage.

♥

IMPOTENCE AND FRIGIDITY:
HOW TO ACHIEVE THEM,
WHOM TO CREDIT, AND WHAT TO SAY

Impotence and frigidity are the classic means by which you can sabotage the act of sex and, ultimately, avoid both love and marriage.

Although you probably put more effort than anybody else into achieving impotence or frigidity, be bigger than your mate— never take all the credit for yourself. Here are some approved remarks to make upon attaining impotence or frigidity:

1. Why did you force me to have those last two martinis?
2. Why did you have to change rhythm on me?
3. Why did you have to talk and ruin my fantasy?
4. Why do you have to make such gross noises?
5. Why did you have to go and beat me at tennis in front of all my friends?
6. Why do you have to be so short?
7. I don't know how you expect me to perform, knowing that you slept with Henry Schmurtz before I met you.

—————————— ♥ ——————————

EXERCISES FOR MEN TO ATTAIN IMPOTENCE

1. Just prior to having sex, concentrate on the thought that your entire reputation as a lover is riding on your next sexual performance. Think of your mate as a drama critic sitting in the seventh row with a note pad and a frown.
2. Just prior to having sex, concentrate on the thought that if you do not achieve erection immediately and maintain it for a minimum of two hours or until your

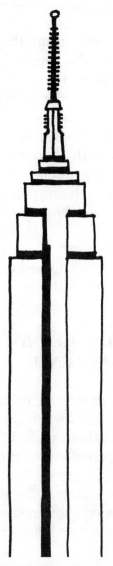

HOW TO TELL
THE DIFFERENCE
BETWEEN THE
ERECT STATE
AND THE
IMPOTENT STATE

THE ERECT STATE   THE IMPOTENT STATE

lover climaxes—whichever is longer—you will lose her.

3. While having sex, concentrate on the thought that all normal, healthy, *heterosexual* men are able to have erections at the drop of a pair of underpants, and if you cannot get one or maintain one it will be proof that you are not a normal, healthy, heterosexual man and should think seriously about becoming a nurse.

♥

EXERCISES FOR WOMEN TO ATTAIN FRIGIDITY

1. While having sex, add up the number of hours you've spent cooking, cleaning, washing dishes, and shopping for groceries while your husband was sleeping, watching TV, or advancing his career.
2. While having sex, add up the number of times your husband has fallen asleep immediately after—or during—lovemaking.
3. While having sex, add up the number of times you've gone to the bathroom in the dark and learned too late that your husband left the toilet seat up.
4. While having sex, imagine that your husband's mother is knocking on your bedroom door, saying: "Sonny, wouldn't you like me to fix you a little bite to eat now?"

FANTASIZING ABOUT OTHERS IN BED

The preceding pages, concerning Impotence and Frigidity, describe how to avoid love and marriage by being absent *physically* during sex. Here's how to be absent *mentally*.

While subjecting yourself to sex with the person you're married to, fantasize that he or she is a well-known movie star. Men, for example, could fantasize about Bo Derek. Women, on the other hand, could fantasize about . . . Bo Derek. It doesn't really matter whom you fantasize about, so long as you fantasize about *somebody*, because the alternative is to be right there in the moment with your mate.

Whatever you do, don't make love to the same person in fantasy on too regular a basis or it will smack of commitment—and that's the *last* thing you need!

HOW TO BECOME INSANELY JEALOUS OF EVERY HUMAN BEING WHO COMES INTO CONTACT WITH YOUR MATE

Nothing drives a wedge between two people as effectively as insane jealousy. Properly utilized, insane jealousy will enable you to stamp out any little sparks of affection that threaten to flare up into marital love.

You may say, "But I'm just not the jealous *type.*" No need to worry. If you follow these simple suggestions, you'll be acting like an insanely jealous idiot in no time at all:

1. Read all of your mate's incoming and outgoing mail.
2. Purchase bugging equipment to keep your mate under surveillance when you can't be there yourself.
3. Call up all your mate's friends and say how upset you are that your mate is having an affair. Wait for them to sympathize with you and spill the beans.
4. At parties, be terribly possessive and rude toward anybody your mate talks to or looks at.
5. Learn the names of your mate's former lovers and send them all death threats.
6. Listen in on all your mate's phone calls, and follow them with confrontations like the example below. (NOTE: This dialogue has been prepared for the Jealous Male, but can easily be adjusted for use by the Jealous Female.)

JEALOUS MALE: "Who was that on the phone, hon?"
MATE: "Just somebody from work."
JEALOUS MALE: "A guy?"
MATE: "Yeah, just some guy from work."
JEALOUS MALE: "Do I know him?"
MATE: "No."
JEALOUS MALE: "Is he cute?"

MATE: "No."

JEALOUS MALE: "He wants to go out with you, doesn't he?"

MATE: "Don't be silly."

JEALOUS MALE: "You want to go to bed with him, don't you?"

MATE: "Give me a break, the guy is a sixty-year-old mail clerk."

JEALOUS MALE: "You've been fooling *around* with this guy, haven't you?"

MATE: "Are you crazy?"

JEALOUS MALE: "Am *I* crazy? I have a wife who's fooling around with a sixty-year-old mail clerk, and *she* asks *me* if *I'm* crazy?"

♥

RULE OF THUMB FOR INSANE JEALOUSY

When you suspect your mate of doing something capable of sending you into a jealous rage, stop. Consider the supposed indiscretion, and then ask yourself the following question: "Would *I* do that?"

If the answer is Yes, then you have every right to become insanely jealous—it is logical to accuse your mate of doing anything of which you yourself might be guilty.

FANNING OLD FLAMES

No subject makes better tinder for marital fights than your mate's former lovers. Lay the groundwork for this by innocently asking your mate for descriptions of his or her former lovers' physical attractiveness, lovemaking prowess, and so on. Then, very skillfully, get your mate to make comparisons between you and these former lovers. For example:

YOU: "That Henry fellow you used to date—he was a pretty attractive guy. How tall do you figure he was, about six-two?"

MATE: "Six-three."

YOU: "Mmmm. He looks really muscular in those old album pictures you showed me."

MATE: "He was all right."

YOU: "He was probably pretty good in bed, huh?"

MATE: "Yeah, sure, he was O.K."

YOU: "What do you mean 'O.K.'?"

MATE: "You know, *O.K.* About average."

YOU: "Am *I* 'O.K.'?"

MATE: "You're fine."

YOU: "What do you mean, 'fine'? Henry's 'O.K.,' and I'm just 'fine'? You know, every time our marriage is going well, you have to throw *Henry* up in my face!"

♥

ADULTERY

You will be tempted many times during the course of your marriage to stray into affairs with friends of the family or kindly strangers. All well and good, so long as you remember *the chief purpose of an extramarital affair is to punish your mate.*

It's imperative that your mate find out about the affair—ideally before you've even consummated it—but how to achieve this?

Let's say you are a man and your intended is a person you flirted with at a dinner party attended by both you and your wife. On returning home, belittle the woman's attractiveness: "Funny thing about that woman Gail I was talking to—from a distance she looks great. But up close she's got large pores and buck teeth."

The other method is to say: "That Gail is sure something, boy—I'd like to eat her underwear." The implication here is that an admiration so boldly stated would never be acted upon.

If you started out by saying this person was a creep, the next time you mention her or him, pretend to forget your previous attitude and talk about how *sexy* you think the person is. Your mate will soon begin to get suspicious.

Feed your mate's suspicions. Come home three or four hours late from work and have a fishy excuse ("I couldn't get a taxi . . . I was mugged . . . I fell asleep at my desk . . . I was abducted by a UFO. . . .") Absentmindedly leave snapshots featuring you and your lover in a place where they might be discovered. Leave a diary out with cryptic but decipherable details of your affair. Come home in a different outfit from the one you left home in. Accidentally call your mate by the wrong name.

Sooner or later, your mate is bound to confront you about it. When this happens, slap your forehead and say: "My God, what gave me away?"

HOW TO TELL IF YOUR MATE IS HAVING SEX WITH SOMEBODY ELSE

If your mate does any of the following, he or she is probably having sex with somebody else:

1. Begins dressing fifteen years younger.
2. Begins dressing up to take out the garbage and is one or two hours late getting back.
3. Begins using unfamiliar expressions in bed like: "Go for it, lover!"

HOW TO TELL IF YOUR MATE IS HAVING SEX ALONE

Is your mate even more uninterested in sex than usual? Does your mate dress up to go to the *bathroom* and not come back for an hour? Have you caught her gently kissing herself on the shoulder or knee or other bodily extremity? Has he or she recently developed acne or hairy palms?

———————— ♥ ————————

TRUE OR FALSE SEX QUIZ

Which of the following statements about sex are true, and which false?

1. The length of a man's sex organ is proportional to the length of his nose.
☐ TRUE ☐ FALSE

2. Whenever you masturbate, the next time you make love you won't be able to achieve orgasm.
☐ TRUE ☐ FALSE

3. If you can't get it up twice in succession, you never will be able to again.
☐ TRUE ☐ FALSE

4. Foreplay is a waste of time.
☐ TRUE ☐ FALSE

5. If you really love your mate, you will be physically attracted to him or her every minute.
☐ TRUE ☐ FALSE

6. If you don't feel like having sex when your mate wants to, you aren't normal.
☐ TRUE ☐ FALSE

7. You only have so many orgasms in you—once you use them up, that's it.

☐ TRUE   ☐ FALSE

Answers:

1. False. The true determinant is his feet.
2. True. It doesn't matter if it's weeks later, either.
3. False. Three times is the critical number.
4. True. A woman is either hot or she's not.
5. True. Varying attraction indicates that it's time to start interviewing potential replacements.
6. True. Normal men and women are always in the mood.
7. True. Men get to have 2,893, women 38.

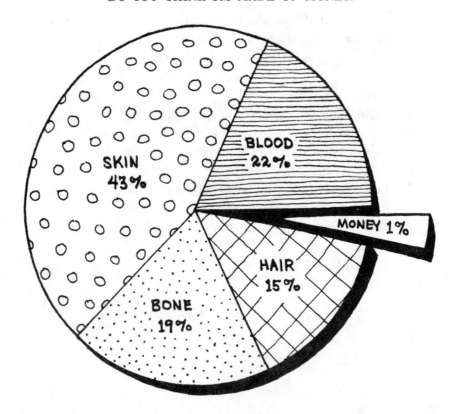

Breakdown of exact chemical composition of your body to show that money is not one of its major components.

Using Money
to Avoid
Love in Marriage

MONEY:
FOR RICHER OR FOR POORER

Money is one of the most fertile areas in which to sow the seeds of marital discord. Just as our international monetary system used to have as its backbone the gold standard, marital monetary systems have a standard of their own known as the *double* standard. In simple terms, the double standard allows for slight discrepancies between your attitude about how *you* spend money and your attitude about how *your mate* spends money.

Let us begin by finding out how much you already know about the use of the double standard of marital money management.

QUIZ ON DOUBLE STANDARD
MARITAL MONEY MANAGEMENT

Decide whether the marital partner in each of the following cases is (A) a sensible money manager or (B) a spendthrift.

1. Your mate goes and buys an 18-karat-gold Rolex watch for him or herself. Your mate is _____
2. Your mate goes out and buys an 18-karat-gold Rolex watch for you as a surprise on your birthday. Your mate is _____.
3. Your business associates are all going skiing in St. Moritz this winter. You reason that if you don't go with them they will think you are hard up for cash, they'll figure that your business is in trouble and stop giving you orders, and pretty soon you'll be filing for bankruptcy. You decide it's imperative to go to St. Moritz, if only to keep up appearances. You are _____.
4. Your mate calculates that by staying home from St. Moritz your finances for the year will be in great shape. Your mate is _____.

Answers:
1. a spendthrift
2. a sensible money manager

3. a sensible money manager
4. a pain in the ass

---------- ♥ ----------

PLANNING FOR YOUR
FINANCIAL FUTURE

In any marriage, there will always be the problem of deciding who makes the budgeting and investment decisions (assuming you have any money left over to invest). But most couples agree that planning for the financial future is imperative. The following are some excellent guidelines:

1. When you marry, insist on registering for twice the number of knives, forks, spoons, and plates that you actually need so that when you split up you will each have a complete set.
2. Vividly label all books, records, posters, and so on with your full name (as it appears on your birth certificate) so that when you get divorced there will be no question which belong to you.
3. Keep a joint checking account and a personal checking account (the latter with a tidy little balance). Pay all bills from the joint checking account.
4. Insist that your mate abandon his or her method of financial record-keeping and adopt yours. Having won that battle:

5. Refuse to file a joint tax return, even if it means paying a higher tax rate. What business is it of your mate's how much you're worth?
6. Try to negotiate a pre-nuptial or post-nuptial agreement outlining who gets how much in the event of a divorce. This may alleviate entirely your need to spend time planning *any* kind of a future together.

WHOSE MONEY IS IT ANYWAY?

In many marriages, one party comes to the union with more financial clout than the other—either because of family money, assets from a previous marriage, or because one partner has a higher-paying job.

If you are the Richer Person:

You are supporting your mate in a style which he or she could never afford without you. Should your mate get any money at all, you obviously assume it's rightfully yours—you're owed it retroactively in return for all that you've spent on your mate.

For example, let's say you owe $8,000 in back taxes. Your mate suddenly inherits, wins, or earns an unexpected lump sum of $8,000. Needless to say, you should expect your mate to use the entire windfall sum to pay your back taxes—after all, you've been supporting him or her, so that money rightfully belongs to you.

Can your mate ever get out of your debt? Of course! Here are two possible methods: (1) by buying out more than half the principal on any mutual holdings; (2) by ruining you financially and making you totally dependent on him or her.

If you are the Poorer Person:

Every month your earnings are so paltry compared to your mate's that you rarely contribute to the enormous monthly overhead. But you reason that two can live as cheaply as one, and that your mate would be paying this overhead whether you were around or not.

Suddenly, your star begins to rise. You earn your first significant chunk of money. You go out and spend $10,000 on a sportscar. Your mate is up in arms. You're furious—it's *your* money, you say, and you'll damn well spend it any way you please.

O'Malley's Law: The Richer Person always thinks that whatever money the Poorer Person has belongs to him.

Greenburg's Corollary: The Poorer Person always expects the Richer Person to take care of him.

"WHO REALLY OWNS THE HOUSE?"
A GAME FOR TWO PLAYERS

In this game there are two positions: Richer Partner and Poorer Partner. If you are the Richer Partner it will be your goal to keep all of the family assets that are already in your name, in your name. Like the house. If you are the Poorer Partner, your goal will be to get the Richer Partner to sign a paper saying that the house that he or she owned previous to the marriage is now half yours.

POORER PARTNER: "You make most of the money in this marriage and I have nothing."

RICHER PARTNER: "Nonsense. Everything I have is yours."

POORER PARTNER: "Even the house?"

RICHER PARTNER: "Well, uh, I did *pay* for the house. But you know it's as much yours as it is mine."

POORER PARTNER: "But it's not really. I don't have a thing on paper that says it's half mine. Why don't we draw up a paper that says it's half mine?"

RICHER PARTNER: "But it's not *fair* for you to own half the house, even though it's half yours."

POORER PARTNER: "If you won't put it on paper, then it's a lie. I don't want to live a lie."

RICHER PARTNER: "Look, the house may be in my name, but as long as we're married it's half yours."

POORER PARTNER: "Oho! So you're planning on a time when we won't be married any longer? Are you planning to leave me?"

RICHER PARTNER: "Am *I* planning to leave *you?* The only reason to put something on paper about owning half the house is if *you're* planning to leave *me.*"

POORER PARTNER: "Well, I wasn't, before this discussion."

RICHER PARTNER: "What's that supposed to mean?"

POORER PARTNER: "That I'm seeing the real you for the first time."

♥

MY MONEY, YOUR MONEY, OUR MONEY

Alas, for many married people, money management is no longer as simple as richer-partner-versus-poorer-partner. Increasingly, marital partners are finding themselves nearly equal in net worth and needing to use more complex formulas for achieving a fair distribution of income and expenses. A currently popular marital accounting system recommends creating three separate categories for marital income and expenses: "My Money," "Your Money," and "Our Money."

Category #1: "My Money": "My Money" is money that belongs to *you*, as opposed to your mate, as in the expression, "This is *my* money—I earned it, it's *mine*."

Naturally, your total personal income should be credited to the "My Money" category. However, to be fair, you'll also want to debit Category #1 for whatever personal expenses you have. For men: cigars, shoeshines, football tickets, mustache wax, toupees, etc. For women: bikini waxes, massages, hairstyling, bubble bath, wrinkle cream, etc.

Category #2: "Your Money": "Your Money" is money that belongs to your mate. Whatever income your mate earns is his or hers, of course. And, like you, your mate will want to pay for the essentials of his or her own upkeep. This includes groceries, telephone, electricity, gas, rent or mortgage, insurance, car repairs, doctor bills, and so on.

Category #3: "Our Money": "Our Money" refers to shared funds. Whatever portion of your mate's salary that remains after paying the expenses in Category #2 is automatically transferred to Category #3.

———————————— ♥ ————————————

THE LIFETIME BALANCE SHEET

Keep a lifetime tally of every single item you and your mate have ever given each other—with dollar values adjusted for contemporary rates of inflation. This will enable you at a moment's notice to inform your mate exactly how much he or she owes you.

FAIR DISTRIBUTION OF SALARIES IN TYPICAL FAMILY BUDGET

FIG. 1: YOUR SALARY

YOUR SHARE   FAMILY'S
                                              SHARE

FIG. 2: MATE'S SALARY

MATE'S   FAMILY'S SHARE
SHARE

ITEM Nº	DATE	DESCRIPTION	CREDIT		DEBIT		MATE'S CURRENT INDEBTEDNESS TO YOU	
9491	12/10	Bought ski parka for mate's Xmas present	210	00			901,647	30
							+210	00
9492	12/12	Bought movie tickets for self and mate	10	00			901,857	30
							+10	00
9493	12/16	Gave mate my dessert	4	25			901,867	30
							+4	25
9494	12/16	Declined sex with mate			7	50	901,871	55
							-7	50
9495	12/17-12/20	Took care of mate during bout of flu	525	00			901,864	05
							+525	00
9496	12/21	Flirted with mate's co-worker at office party			27	25	902,389	05
							-27	25
9497	12/22	Bought mate video game with 3 cassettes	359	95			902,361	80
							+359	95
9498	12/25	Was kind to in-laws at Xmas dinner	400	00			902,721	75
							+400	00
9499	12/26	Grouchy to mate due to hangover			5	15	903,121	75
							-5	15

SAMPLE OF TYPICAL LIFETIME BALANCE SHEET

♥

TEST PROBLEM:
COOKING IN VS. EATING OUT

Problem:

According to your husband's way of thinking, when he takes you out to Dinner in a Nice Restaurant (D.N.R.) at his expense, that is equivalent to 34 Dinners that you Cook for him at Home (D.C.H.). Or, expressed as a formula:

$$1 \text{ D.N.R.} = 34 \text{ D.C.H.}$$

Your husband now invites you to spend a week with him in Barbados. Assuming that he equates a Week in the Caribbean (W.C.) with 617 Dinners in Nice Restaurants (D.N.R.), how many Dinners will you have to Cook for him at Home (D.C.H.) before you are out of his debt for this vacation?

Solution:

You will have to cook 20,978 dinners for him at home, which is not possible if you are over 15 years old.

An even more promising issue for promoting marital discord through money is renovating houses. In the following quiz you will get a chance to see whether this exciting area is right for *you*.

RENOVATION QUIZ

You and your mate are contemplating a renovation of your house. You have limited funds. In the following list, try to figure out which choices you would make and which your mate would make. Then consult the key at the end of the quiz to see what you should do.

1. Your family-room sofa has begun to look a little the worse for wear. Would you:
   (a) Reupholster it in an attractive new fabric? Or:
   (b) Throw a sheet over it and tuck in the sides?

2. Your refrigerator still works, but it lacks the zip of the newer models. Would you:
   (a) Buy a new double-door refrigerator with an automatic ice cube maker? Or:
   (b) Keep the existing model, but spray paint it an interesting color and splurge on new ice trays?

3. The floors in your house are worn out. Would you:
   (a) Put in parquet flooring throughout? Or:
   (b) Put in linoleum?

4. Your toilet is perfectly functional, but rather old and discolored. Would you:
   (a) Buy a stylish new toilet with a low silhouette? Or:

(b) Keep your old toilet, but buy a fake-fur seat cover for it?

5. Your back yard is large enough for a swimming pool and you've both always wanted one. Would you:
   (a) Build a big pool with a diving board? Or:
   (b) Get a 12-foot-diameter above-the-ground vinyl wading pool?

Key:

If you and your mate both chose mostly A's, you have similar tastes and will have a satisfying, if costly renovation. If you and your mate chose mostly B's, don't renovate. If one of you chose A's, and the other chose B's, you have a further choice: either don't renovate, or don't stay married.

———————— ♥ ————————

MULTIPLE CHOICE TEST
ON FURNITURE SHOPPING

You and your mate are shopping for couches or modular seating arrangements. You prefer very traditional furniture, especially antiques. Your mate sees a starkly modern Italian couch to which you take an instant loathing. Your mate announces that he or she is going to buy it. Should you:

(a) Explain to your mate that the starkly modern Italian couch will be inconsistent with the rest of the decor in your home?

(b) Say that, while you admire the piece in and of itself, it doesn't exactly suit your taste, and perhaps there is another couch that your mate can find that will be more of a compromise?

(c) Burst into tears?

Answer: C, of course.

———————— ♥ ————————

THE MONEY TEST

Question:

What is the optimum amount of money you and your mate need to earn per year in order to be happily married?

1. $25,000
2. $75,000
3. $500,000
4. $1,000,000, tax-free

Answer:

What makes you think that you are ever going to be happily married?

Using Fighting
to Avoid
Love in Marriage

♥

WHY YOU NEED TO FIGHT

Let's face it, your marriage hasn't turned out the way it was supposed to, the way that marriages have always been portrayed in songs and movies. Well, there's nothing to be done about it. You have once again gotten the short end of the stick, once more been cheated out of the good things in life. But you probably have to put up with it, because it's no more than you deserve.

One way of expressing your disillusionment is by picking fights* with your mate. Fighting is a good way to make sure you

---

* It is important to point out here that other married couples don't fight. Or, if they do, it's never as ugly as the fights that you and your mate have. It's vital that nobody in the world find out that you fight or that your marriage is anything but perfect.

and your mate don't get any closer. It is also a great way to get out anger and hostility that you might feel towards somebody less safe to yell at, like your boss. On the succeeding pages you will learn the ABC's of marital fighting—vocabulary, pronunciation, style, syntax—in short, every tool you'll ever need to keep your mate from getting too close to you.

Where To Fight

Why trivialize something as important as a marital fight by having it just any place at all, any time at all? Expensive French restaurants are ideal settings for marital fights. Shedding tears into a flaming pan of crêpes suzette in an expensive French restaurant is much more dramatic than sniveling into a smoking pot of burnt Chef Boy-ar-dee lasagne at home. And after causing an ugly scene in a public place, there is the added value of walking out in the middle of dinner, leaving over one hundred dollars worth of gourmet food.

If you're unable to afford expensive French restaurants as a place to stage your marital fights, the home of your in-laws is an acceptable alternative.

When To Fight

When *is* the best time to have a marital fight? The answer is any time at all. Have a marital fight while your mate is trying to shave, work, balance a checkbook, or fall asleep. But to get the most out of your marital fight, arrange to have it on an occasion as auspicious as an anniversary, a birthday, Thanksgiving, Christmas, Easter, New Year's Eve, New Year's Day, or during any romantic occasion in a foreign country.

———————————— ♥ ————————————

FIVES RULES TO GOVERN MARITAL FIGHTS

No matter how emotional the argument you may be having with your mate, the depth of your relationship demands that you keep the following five rules in mind: (1) Reason with your mate. (2) Acknowledge your mate's expertise. (3) Acknowledge your mate's worth. (4) Point out your *own* worth. (5) Give your mate an opportunity to explain.

Here are illustrations of the foregoing:

1. *Reasoning with your mate:*
   "Just give me one good *reason* why I should listen to you."
2. *Acknowledging your mate's expertise:*
   "Tell me about it—*you're* the expert."
3. *Acknowledging your mate's worth:*
   "I'm sorry I'm not perfect like *you* are."
4. *Pointing out your own worth:*
   "After I'm dead and buried, you'll realize I wasn't so terrible."

5. *Giving your mate an opportunity to explain:*
"Are you deliberately trying to destroy me, or are you just the most inconsiderate person in the world?"

Now that you've learned the rules, it's time to build a vocabulary to utilize in marital fights.

♥

BUILDING YOUR OWN FIGHTING SENTENCES

You are ready to begin building your own sentences to fight with. To help you on your way, here is a pronunciation guide to some of the most popular fighting phrases:

1. ĭ mō′ shŭn ŭl blăk′ māl′
2. ĭ mō′ shŭn ŭl krĭp′ ŭl′
3. ĭ mō′ shŭn ŭl ĭ băngk′ rŭpt
4. môr′ ŭ lĭ băngk′ rŭpt
5. när′ sĭs ĭs′ tĭk chīld′
6. sĕk′ sĭst pĭg′
7. ĭ măs′ kyŭ lā tĭng bĭch′
8. joi′ lĭs wûr′ kŭ hôl′ ĭk
9. kăr′ ĭk tŭr ŭ să′ sĭ nā′ shŭn
10. pĕn′ ĭ pĭn′ chĭng băs′ tŭrd
11. kŭt′ ĭng ôf′ mī lĭfs′ blŭd′

12. drī′ vĭng ŭ stāk′ thrū mī härt′

13. mā′ kĭng mĭ ĭn′ tū ŭ shrĭl pă′ rŭ dĭ ŭv mī sĕlf′

Practice saying the above phrases aloud in private. When you feel you've mastered them, you may proceed to our next section, where you will learn a number of complete sentences you can use in actual marital fights of your own.

♥

A LEXICON FOR
FIGHTING MARITAL FIGHTS,
ARRANGED ACCORDING TO SUBJECT

Amnesia: "Who do you think you *are?*"

Apology: "Pardon me for *living!*"

Autobiography: "I've spent the best years of my life with you— and for *what?*"

Barter: "I don't have to take this from you."

Courage: "You don't have the *guts* to leave me."

Dancing: "You just waltz in here and you think you *own* the place."

Exercise: "Go ahead and *throw* it, if you think it will make you *feel* better."

Family tree: "She's *your* mother, not mine."

Hearing impairments: "Could you speak up a little? They can't hear you in Europe."

Illness: "You make me sick." (*Advanced illness:* "The mere thought of spending one more night with you is enough to make me sick.")

Language barrier: "What's the matter, don't you understand English?"

Military: "You're really out of line."

Mining: "I hadn't realized we'd descended to that level."

Myopia: "I'm seeing the real you for the first time."

Oceanography: "How low can you possibly sink?"

Ready-to-wear: "How did I get *into* this?"

Refrigeration: "You always spoil everything."

Reportage: "I've got *news* for you."

Talent: "Boy, you're some little actor, aren't you?"

Wildlife: "That's right, use physical violence. That's all an animal like you knows anyway."

FIGHTING: STYLE AND SYNTAX

Anything you say in a marital fight will have more bounce if you utilize a melodramatic style and an archaic syntax. A statement like "I'm sorry I ever met you" is effective enough, but how much more piquant is the same communication expressed as: "I *rue the day* I met you."

Calling your mate a "jerk" or a "turkey" is a little vapid compared to calling him a *scoundrel*. Observing that something your mate did was "mean" pales beside remarking that it was *heinous* or *dastardly*. Asking whether your mate has time for a discussion is tapioca pudding compared with asking whether your mate *would deign to favor you* with his or her attention.

Enough of pronunciation, vocabulary, style,* and syntax— now on to an actual fight!

HOW TO START A FIGHT
IN ANY SITUATION

The experienced professional should be able to pick a fight with a mate over anything at all, any time at all. This is an acquired talent, to be sure, but one not totally out of your grasp. Let's

---

* NOTE: For further guidance in style, refer back to p. 40 and the techniques of Mimicking.

look at a few examples of what can be done with innocuous remarks about the weather:

Example A

MATE: "Nice day."

YOU: "Oh, yeah? What's nice about it?"

Example B

MATE: "Hot enough for you?"

YOU: "What's *that* supposed to mean—that it has to be hotter for me than for other people?"

Example C

MATE: "Think it's going to rain?"

YOU: "What the hell am I supposed to be, a goddam *weatherman*, for chrissakes?"

Example D

MATE: "We sure could use some rain."

YOU: "We could use a *lot* of things that *you* couldn't supply if your *life* depended on it."

But, you may say, the above examples are not really *provocative* enough to sustain a fight of any satisfying duration. Read on!

---------- ♥ ----------

HOW TO TURN AN ORDINARY DISCUSSION INTO A FIGHT OF SATISFYING DURATION

At any point in an otherwise lackluster discussion, you might introduce the following sure-fire provocative questions:

1. "So in other words you don't think I'm masculine/feminine?" (Choose one.)
2. "Then what are you saying, that I'm a coward?"
3. "What are you trying to say, that you think I'm not good in bed?"
4. "Are you trying to tell me that you find him/her more attractive than I am?"

---------- ♥ ----------

TEST PROBLEM: SHARING THE COOKING

Your husband steadfastly refuses to help out in the kitchen. Following several ugly fights on the subject, he has vowed to do his share of the cooking from now on. He invites his boss and

1 can cheese ravioli in sauce
1 can opener
1 gas range
1 large saucepan

1 large spoon
1 large plate or bowl
1 pot holder or equivalent

1. Place can of ravioli in opener. Gently squeeze handles together until you hear a soft popping sound. Then gently but firmly turn revolving crank in a clockwise direction until the lid of the tin is almost but not quite separated from the body of the can.

2. Preheat your large saucepan under low flame. Briskly fold contents of can into saucepan, stirring with your large spoon. A covered saucepan will heat more rapidly than an uncovered one.

3. While ravioli is simmering, take out a clean bowl or plate and hold it in readiness. It does not pay to take your bowl or plate out either too soon or too late. Too soon, and you risk cluttering up your work area with unnecessary utensils. Too late, and you risk pouring steaming ravioli onto your counter.

4. When ravioli is thoroughly heated, remove saucepan from flame, grasping handle with pot holder, baking mitt, or asbestos welder's glove. Pour contents of saucepan into preset bowl or plate until saucepan is empty.

5. Garnish with spoons, forks, knives, and napkins.

COMPLETE INSTRUCTIONS FOR HUSBAND WHO HAS FINALLY PROMISED
TO SHARE THE COOKING TO MAKE A TASTY ITALIAN DINNER

several business associates to dinner but, conveniently, has to go out to run some errands when it's time to begin preparations for the meal.

Should you:
- *(A)* Start dinner now and ask your husband to help when he gets home?
- *(B)* Wait to start dinner until your husband is ready to do his share?

Answer:

If you keep your wits about you, you can make either option work for you. Let's see how.

Option A:
Begin preparing dinner now, fuming about what a liar, hypocrite, and opportunistic male chauvinist pig your husband is. When he returns home, refuse to ask him to help. In fact, refuse to acknowledge that he is even there. Throughout the dinner party, never speak to him directly, but use one of the guests—preferably your husband's boss—as an interpreter: "Mr. Winer, could you please ask my husband if it would be too much trouble for him to pass the butter?"

Option B:
You know your husband will *never* be ready to do his share. Don't do your share either. When your guests sit down at the

dinner table and your husband asks, "Say, hon, what's for dinner?," explain that you were just about to ask him the same question. What with his boss there and all, you will be able to Teach Him a Lesson He Will Never Forget.

The above situation, however it's resolved, should never be forgotten. It is, in fact, an excellent opportunity to start a truly valuable and satisfying collection of Marital Grievances.

───────────── ♥ ─────────────

COLLECTING GRIEVANCES

Begin a list of grievances—things your mate has said or done, or failed to say or do—and keep it active, replenishing the supply on a daily basis. This list will be the raw material you need for really satisfying marital fights. If you didn't have this list to refer to, you might forget all the things your mate has done to victimize you. In time you will have to get revenge for everything on that list.

Collecting grievances is like collecting stamps, coins, butterflies, or anything else. Start modestly and you will soon be able to recognize really first-class specimens when they come along, and your collection will be the envy of all your friends.

But, you say, where do I start? My mate, you say, is a wonderful person and there is nothing I can think of to resent. This is a poor attitude and shows a paucity of imagination. What about starting your list with several things you can't do anymore be-

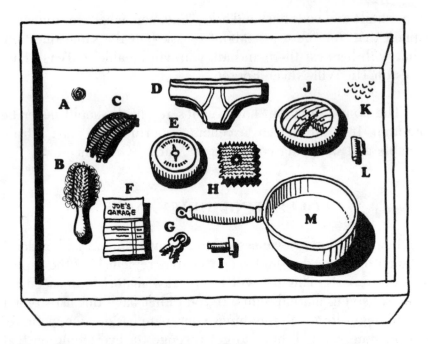

DISPLAY CASE FOR MARITAL GRIEVANCE COLLECTION

A. Hair from bathtub drain which your mate *never* removes. **B.** Your hairbrush, once more clogged with mate's hair. **C.** Black bananas which mate let go bad in kitchen again. **D.** Mate's soiled underwear, *continually* left on floor. **E.** Thermostat which mate always insists on setting either too low or too high. **F.** Bill for road service when mate forgot to fill up tank and you ran out of gas in the middle of nowhere. **G.** House keys mate left at home, when you *specifically* said you weren't taking yours. **H.** Section of your favorite coat, burnt by mate's cigarette. **I.** Your safety razor, which mate has ruined after vowing not to use it anymore. **J.** Headlight mate shattered by misjudging depth of garage. **K.** Toenail clippings mate left in carpet again. **L.** Cap of your favorite pen which mate thoughtlessly left in restaurant. **M.** Saucepan encrusted with burnt food that mate left for *you* to clean, which is typical.

cause you're married—like hang out with your chums or have dates with really exciting partners?

See how easy it is? Here is a starter list of grievances to get you into the swing of things:

1. He always flushes the toilet when I'm in the shower and scalds me.
2. She snores and insists she doesn't.
3. He brushes his teeth and clears his throat and spits phlegm into the sink along with the toothpaste.
4. She clutters up the whole bathtub ledge with bottles of cream rinse, and the shower curtain bar with drying lingerie.
5. He refuses to learn how to operate the washing machine, the drier, the oven, etc., because he considers all household chores to be exclusively my domain.
6. She's always rushing me to leave the house for social engagements, but is never ready herself.
7. He refuses to cover food in the refrigerator, and it dries up and becomes inedible. Plus, he forgets to eat his bananas and they get black and rotten and I have to throw them out or make banana bread.
8. She refuses to take a coat or sweater to air-conditioned theaters in the summer. She gets cold and asks to borrow mine, and then I have to give it to her and *I'm* the one who freezes.

9. He starts reading any magazine or newspaper or book I bring home and then won't give it back.
10. She never tells me where things are in the house when I ask her, especially if I've already asked her where six or seven things are. I think she hides them.
11. He is always asking where things are, even if they're his things and he put them wherever they are—he won't even *try* to look for them before asking me because he thinks he's some kind of prince and I have to wait on him hand and foot.
12. She expects me to help with the dishes and the cooking, even though I put in a hard day of work at the office and all she has to do is lie around the house during the day and do maybe a little light dusting.
13. He always asks my opinion on things and then gets mad when I give it.

Got the idea? Now you're ready for a slightly more sophisticated notion:

———— ♥ ————

OBSCURE GRIEVANCES

It is not essential that all grievances against your mate be rational. For example, it is wholly appropriate to hold your mate responsible for things that he or she does to you in *dreams.*

It is also appropriate to hold your mate responsible for terrible things you imagine that he or she might do to you at some time in the future.

YOU: "Honey?"

MATE: "Yes, dear?"

YOU: "If I were sick in the hospital, would you walk out on me?"

MATE: "Of *course* not. What kind of a silly question is that?"

YOU: "I mean if I were *really* sick. If I were in an accident, say, and I lost a couple of toes. Would you walk out on me *then*?"

MATE: "A couple of *toes*? Of *course* not. What kind of silly questions are these anyway?"

YOU: "What if I lost a couple of toes, two legs, two arms, and my face was disfigured beyond recognition. Would you walk out on me *then*?"

(PAUSE)

MATE: "Well, uh, we'd have to *see*. I mean, uh, I certainly wouldn't be in a position to, uh———"

YOU: "I *knew* it—you *never* loved me! You're just waiting for *any* excuse to walk out on me!"

MORE OBSCURE GRIEVANCES

Here are some additional Obscure Grievances which, although farfetched, you probably already have in your collection:

1. Your mate's height.
2. Your mate's ability (or lack of ability) to fall asleep.
3. Your mate's astrological sign.
4. That your mate puts the toilet-paper roll in upside down.
5. That your mate had other lovers before you met.
6. That your mate might remarry if you die first.

♥

COMPLETION GAME:
FILL-IN-THE-GRIPE

Let's see how much you've learned so far. You have 30 seconds to complete the following test. Ready . . . Get set . . . Start.

1. "How dare you _____?"
2. "That's right, just go right ahead and _____!"
3. "What do you think you're _____?"
4. "Where did I ever get the idea that you _____?"
5. "Why do you always have to be so damned _____?"

DISPLAY CASE FOR *OBSCURE* MARITAL GRIEVANCE COLLECTION

A. Keys to sportscar you had to sell to buy stationwagon when you had your first child, although you didn't want kids in the first place. **B.** Love letter from person you dropped for present mate, with whom, in hindsight, you had lots more fun and lots more passion. **C.** Calendar with days marked off on which your mate failed to surprise you with an extravagant romantic gesture. **D.** I.D. bracelet given to mate by high school sweetheart whom mate probably loved more than you. **E.** Travel brochures describing places you could have afforded to visit if you were still single. **F.** Musical instrument you played in high school band which, if you weren't saddled with the responsibilities of marriage, you might now be playing in the New York Philharmonic. **G.** Snapshot of extremely attractive person whom your mate would hop into the sack with in a *minute*, if they ever met. **H.** Insurance company actuarial tables listing age your mate will die and leave you all alone, after you're too old and unattractive to find another partner.

6. "After all I've done for you, I really deserve _____!"

7. "Not once in this whole discussion have I heard you say _____!"

8. "In all my life I've never seen such _____!"

9. "It's clear to me that our entire relationship _____!"

10. "Is it too much to ask to _____?"

11. "I'd pay any amount of money to _____!"

12. "That's the last time I ever _____!"

13. "I don't suppose it's ever occurred to you that ____?"

14. "I suppose you think you can just _____?"

15. "I see now what a fool I was to _____!"

16. "I've had it up to here with your _____!"

17. "I've spent the best years of my life _____!"

18. "If I didn't have you, I'd be able to _____!"

19. "If I hear you say that one more time _____!"

20. "If you could just shut up long enough to _____!"

21. "If I've told you once, I've told you a million times _____!"

22. "If I hadn't wasted so much time on you already _____!"

23. "If anybody had told me this was how I'd be spending my _____!"

24. "If you have even so much as a spark of decency left in your body, you'll _____!"

25. "If you _____ once more, you'll regret it!"

26. "If you think ＿＿＿＿＿＿＿＿＿, you've got another thought coming!"

27. "That may be how you talk to your ＿＿＿＿＿ at the ＿＿＿＿＿, but that's not how you're going to talk to *me!*"

28. "And to think I chose you instead of ＿＿＿＿＿!"

To help you in the complex area of marital fights we strongly recommend consultation with a good marital counselor or psychotherapist. For some of the benefits to be gained from such a source, consult the following section.

———————— ♥ ————————

THE BENEFITS OF THERAPY

If you happen to have experience with Freudian analysis, group psychotherapy, est, or some other form of training, your communications to your mate during marital squabbles will be considerably enhanced.

For example, if you happen to be in therapy, here are some phrases you might use:

1. "My psychiatrist says you're inhibiting me."

2. "My shrink says I'm not supposed to let you talk to me like that."

3. "Nobody in my group has these kinds of problems with *their* husbands."

4. "My group thinks you're an emotional *retard*."

5. "My therapist thinks you're a wimp."

You will also be able to utilize the special words and phrases you have learned in therapy. Your mate will find these particularly grating. For example:

1. "Will you stop *acting out* and start *relating?*"

2. "You know what this is about? *Transference.*"

3. "What's the psychological *payoff* in all this for you?"

4. "Boy, do you have a lot of *repressed rage.*"

5. "You're a classic example of *anal-retentive* behavior."

As effective as these phrases are if *you* learned them in therapy, they will be geometrically more grating if it's not you but your *mate* who learned them in therapy and you *co-opted* them. In this case you can add such statements as:

1. "I wish Dr. Zitzfleisch could hear you now."

2. "Just a minute, I'm going to get Dr. Zitzfleisch on the phone so you can *repeat* that for him."

3. "If that's all you got out of seven years of therapy with Dr. Zitzfleisch, you wasted your money."

If your mate has been in est or has recently spent time in California, here are some approved sentences to use:

1. "I get that you're having an *up*set."
2. "Don't go into *over*whelm on me."
3. "Why don't you stop running your *tape* on me?"
4. "I need my own *space*."
5. "That's a big *with*hold."
6. "That's a big *make*-wrong."
7. "I want you to get *clear* that I'm your wife and not your *mother*."
8. "I'd just like to *share* that I think you're an *asshole*."

Enough of therapy. It is high time we taught you some fighting strategy. For example, do you know at what point in a marital fight to admit you're wrong?

---------- ♥ ----------

ADMITTING YOU'RE WRONG

When you are having an argument with your mate, *never* admit you're wrong. Admitting you're wrong is a sign of weakness—or worse. If you admit you're wrong about anything, you start a dangerous trend—you leave yourself open to the possibility that you could be found wrong at any time in the future. This is something you cannot afford, so make this slogan your watchword:

"I'd rather be right than married."

Now then, how to prove that you are right and your mate is wrong? By Assigning Blame.

HOW TO ASSIGN BLAME

Where there's trouble, there is Blame. Blame Is the Name of the Game. *Every single phenomenon in the entire universe is somebody's fault.* The only way to absolve yourself of blame is to prove that it was somebody *else's* fault.

But what if whatever it is really *was* your fault? What to do then, admit it? Perish the thought. If you have been knowingly wrong in any matter involving your mate, the only way to correct this uncomfortable situation is to rationalize that your mate deserved whatever it was, and you are totally absolved.

This technique is known as Retroactive Deserving. Let's see how it works.

RETROACTIVE DESERVING

Let's say you borrowed your mate's sweater and somehow got it stained and dirty. You take it to a cleaner and the cleaner tells you the stains are permanent and the garment is ruined.

Resist the temptation to feel bad. Feeling bad will not get the stains out of the sweater, will it? It will not. All right, then. The only important thing is to get you to stop feeling bad. Would you feel bad if the sweater was already permanently stained when you borrowed it? You would not.

Try to think: *Was* the sweater permanently stained when

you borrowed it? Perhaps it wasn't. *But perhaps it wasn't absolutely 100 percent spanking clean either.* Perhaps it was just slightly soiled. Isn't that possible? Doesn't that strike a responsive chord in your memory? It does, doesn't it? And you know the reason it does? *Because, deep down, you know that your mate is really a slob.*

So if your mate is such a slob, what difference does it make whether you've stained the sweater or not? If your mate is such a slob, maybe the stains on the sweater won't even be *noticed.*

Better yet, if your mate is such a slob, he or she *deserves* to have you stain that sweater. In fact, why not go and look at the messy state your mate's clothes are in right now and mess them up a little more.

(NOTE: This technique of Retroactive Deserving can also be used to rationalize a number of useful and interesting activities, like jumping into bed with someone other than your mate.)

Now that you have learned the valuable skills of Assigning Blame and Retroactive Deserving, you are ready to proceed to the highly sophisticated techniques of Punishing Your Mate.

♥

HOW TO PUNISH YOUR MATE

There are many ways to punish your mate after the major dialogue of a marital fight is over. One speaks here of punishment for past, present, and even future grievances. Some of these methods are:

1. Sulking.
2. Pouting.
3. Soft crying. (This need not be limited to women.)
4. Never enjoying yourself.
5. Avoiding sex.
6. Avoiding touching at all.
7. Turning to drink.
8. Getting fired.
9. Getting sick. (See Sickness as Punishment, p. 120.)
10. Having affairs.
11. The Silent Treatment.

♥

THE SILENT TREATMENT

How does it work? When to use it? How to handle necessary communications and not risk having your mate think that you are being friendly?

The Silent Treatment is an excellent method of punishing your mate and extending fights for hours, days, weeks—yes, even *years!* The Silent Treatment* includes the above-mentioned techniques of sulking, pouting, soft crying, not touching, and so on, but demands the sort of discipline usually found in Trappist monks. If you do not have this sort of discipline, this technique

---

* The Silent Treatment is also an effective technique for letting your mate know you have something on your mind.

can be modified to General Silence with Exaggerated Politeness, and Pretending Not to Hear or Understand Whatever Is Said to One. For example:

"I beg your pardon, were you addressing *me?*"
Or:
"I'm so dreadfully sorry, did you *say* something?"

Ultimately, however, it is to your advantage to find the little pockets of smoldering anger left over from the conflagration—"extensions" is what the fire department calls them—and fan these until they burst once more into a nice reassuring blaze.

How long you stick with The Silent Treatment depends upon how much your mate deserves it. A Philadelphia woman became so furious with her husband on a cruise to the Virgin Islands that when she accidentally fell overboard she wouldn't even give him the satisfaction of calling out for help. She never spoke to her husband—or anybody else—ever again.

And now a final quiz on punishing your mate:

QUIZ ON THE SILENT TREATMENT

Which of the following is *not* a legitimate technique in The Silent Treatment?

1. Avoiding touching your mate
2. Sulking

3. Soft crying
4. Pouting
5. Praying
6. Fellatio

♥

SICKNESS AS PUNISHMENT

One of the most effective ways of punishing your mate is to make yourself sick. If you say that this isn't an acceptable form of punishment because you will suffer more than your mate, you are not a serious person and have learned nothing so far in this book.

Now then, how to make yourself sick? There are a number of ways: Hold in your rage. Brood about how horribly and how unfairly your mate treats you until you develop a pain in your stomach, your head, or your heart. Once you have succeeded in getting these pains, go to the library, take out medical books listing the symptoms of a number of dread diseases, and see how many of these you already have and which ones you will need to develop.

Only serious diseases are effective punishments. To imply that your mate has given you a headache or dandruff or stomach gas is small potatoes. To make your punishment effective, go for one of the biggies—a disease that will require long and expensive medical treatments, like embolisms or malignancies.

If you succeed in contracting one of these, you will probably

BIRDSEYE VIEW OF COUPLE IN BED AFTER
MARITAL FIGHT.
WHICH PARTNER, A OR B,
IS GIVING THE OTHER THE SILENT TREATMENT?

be letting yourself in for a great deal of pain and, ultimately, death. But just think of what revenge it will be on your mate!

If you are not successful in contracting a terminal disease, you could always commit suicide—but only after you've threatened it till your mate no longer takes you seriously.

------------------------------- ♥ -------------------------------

PACKING FOR DRAMATIC EFFECT

Some people feel cheated if their mates don't appear to be taking their fights seriously. The more they scream and cry and throw things, the more their partners become involved in reading the newspaper or watching TV.

This, incidentally, is not a bad little tactic, but how to counter it? One way is to dramatize the importance of the fight by going to the closet, taking down a couple of suitcases, and loudly beginning to pack.* Don't be deterred by sarcastic comments from your mate like: "Going out for Chinese food, hon?" However cool your mate is playing it, underneath, he or she is really sweating.

If you persist in packing, your mate will ultimately acknowledge you by saying in a totally innocent tone: "Hey, is there something wrong?"

One word of caution is in order, however. It is vital to know how far to go. Should you actually pick up your packed suitcases

* NOTE: The new soft luggage makes it considerably harder to pack loudly. You might try loudly zipping and unzipping the industrial zippers.

and go all the way to the front door? Should you open the door? Go down the steps? Get into your car or hail a cab? How obvious will it be that you have no place to go? At what point, if any, can your mate be counted upon to stop you?

— ♥ —

MAKING UP

Before considering any course of action as drastic as making up after a fight, stop a moment and think. Are you being too hasty? Are you acting in the heat of passion and committing yourself to something you're going to be sorry for later?

If you are *still* determined to make up, here are some points to consider:

1. The person who *started* the fight must be the one to end it.
2. The person who was *wrong* must be the one to end it.
3. If the person who *started* the fight and the person who was *wrong* are not the same person, the fight can never be ended.

— ♥ —

HOW TO TELL WHO STARTED IT

The person who first raised his or her voice above conversational level is probably the one who started it. Although deciding precisely what "conversational level" is, especially if you don't own a decibel meter, is a little tricky. Suffice it to say that the person who threw the first ashtray was probably the one who started it.

HOW TO TELL WHO WAS WRONG

This one is much easier. The person who is *not you* is the one who was probably wrong.

WHAT TO DO NEXT

All right, let's say you've determined who started it and who was wrong. Does that mean you are now irrevocably locked into making up? Not necessarily. You still have options. Here are a few of them:

1. Pretend not to hear your mate admitting fallibility or agreeing to make up. Belabor the point in question and refuse to let your mate off the hook.
2. Pretend to make up, but don't forgive your mate, and file the grievance away for future use.
3. Start to make up and, just before the embrace, pull away with a bitter remark.

4. Refuse your mate's apology, saying it's too late for that now.
5. Offer an apology yourself which cannot be accepted.

HOW TO OFFER
AN UNACCEPTABLE APOLOGY

This skill is a crucial one in all marital fights. It is a two-part process: (1) Start out with an acceptable initial statement, then (2) follow it up with one that invalidates it.

For example:

(A) "O.K., I'm wrong. (PAUSE) Funny how *I'm* always the one who's wrong."

(B) "I'm sorry, honey, I don't know why I said such awful things to you. (PAUSE) Even though they're true."

(C) "All right, I apologize. (PAUSE) O.K.? You *satisfied* now? O.K.?"

CONCLUDING THE FIGHT

At some point in the altercation—certainly not before 4:00 a.m.—you may run out of vile things to say to each other. Your

APOLOGY CARD FOR THE AMBIVALENT

throat is dry, you are hoarse, and you're so tired you can barely keep your eyes open. But how to end it? What are the words you can use to bring the whole sordid mess to some sort of conclusion?

Here are a number of suggestions that have been found effective:

1. "Since you obviously don't care what I think, I just won't speak anymore."
2. "Since everything I do is wrong, I just won't do anything anymore."
3. "I've had it, that's all I can take, I just can't take it anymore."
4. "I'm fed up, I've had my fill, I'm fed up to *here*."
5. "If that's the way you feel, we might just as well end it."
6. "I guess we're just not meant to be together."
7. "You do what *you* have to do, I'll do what *I* have to do."
8. "I guess I'm just not the man/woman for you."
9. "There's nothing more for us to discuss."
10. "You won't have (YOUR NAME GOES HERE) to kick around anymore."

♥

MULTIPLE CHOICE TEST
ON DIVORCE

In which of the situations described below—if any—is it appropriate to pronounce the phrase "I want a divorce"?

(A) You and your mate are having an emotional fight.
(B) You have discovered that your mate is having an affair.
(C) You have discovered that *you* are having an affair.
(D) You are both having tremendous cash flow problems.
(E) You woke up with a headache.

Answer: All of the above.

♥

EMERGENCY INTERNATIONAL
MULTILINGUAL PHRASEBOOK AND
PRONUNCIATION GUIDE
FOR MARITAL PARTNERS

ENGLISH: I want a divorce.
          (eye wunt uh duh-VORS)
SPANISH: Yo quiero un divorcio.
          (yo KYEH-ro oon dee-VOR-see-oh)

SPLITTING UP: WHO GETS WHAT?

ITALIAN:	Io voglio divorziare.
	(EE-oh VOL-yo dee-vor-SA-ray)
FRENCH:	Je veux divorcer.
	(zheh vuh dee-vor-SAY)
GERMAN:	Ich will eine Ehescheidung.
	(ich vil EYE-nuh ay-uh-SHY-doonk)
RUSSIAN:	Я ХОЧУ РАЗВОД
	(ya-ha-CHOO ross-VOD)
POLISH:	Ya chce rozwod.
	(ya ch-TZEN ross-VOD)
FINNISH:	Minä halvan avioeron.
	(MEE-nah HOLL-wan AH-vee-oh-AIR-on)
HEBREW:	אני רוצה גט.
	(ah-NEE ro-TZEH get)
YIDDISH:	איך וויל אגט.
	(ich vill ah-GET)

A FINAL WORD

We have taught you how to avoid commitment and keep your options open, even during an ongoing marriage. You have learned how to use sex, money, and fighting to ward off intimacy and prevent the discomfort of getting too close.

You now have all the tools you will ever need to avoid love and marriage. If you have enjoyed this book, you will want to be on the lookout for our next one, *How to Get the Most Pain Out of Your Divorce.*

This book has been dedicated to:
Kip & Linda
Keith & Laurie
Denise & Michael
Lee & Jan
Bob & Merrilee
Sylvia & Mark
Kathy & Steve
Irma & Don
Mary Ann & Grace

Books by Dan Greenburg

What Do Women Want?
Love Kills
Something's There
Scoring
Porno-graphics
Philly
Jumbo the Boy and Arnold the Elephant
Chewsday
How to Make Yourself Miserable
Kiss My Firm But Pliant Lips
How to Be a Jewish Mother

ABOUT THE AUTHORS

Suzanne O'Malley, a former Senior Editor of *Esquire* Magazine, was raised in Dallas and is a Phi Beta Kappa Graduate of the University of Texas at Austin. Her reviews and articles have appeared in *The New York Times Magazine, The New York Times Book Review, Esquire, Playboy, Ms., Glamour,* and *Cosmopolitan.* She currently lives in New York City and co-wrote the screenplay for Universal Pictures' *Private School* with her husband, Dan Greenburg.

Dan Greenburg was born and raised in Chicago and received his B.A. from the University of Illinois and his M.A. from U.C.L.A. His writings have appeared in *The New Yorker, Esquire, Playboy, Life, Ms., The New York Times Magazine,* and *The New York Times Book Review. His How to Be a Jewish Mother* made *Publishers Weekly's* list of the 25 best-selling non-fiction titles of all time. His other best-sellers include *What Do Women Want?, Love Kills, Scoring,* and *How To Make Yourself Miserable.* A resident of New York City, he wrote the screenplay for *Private Lessons* and co-wrote the screenplay for *Private School* with his wife, Suzanne O'Malley.